In my eighth decade
& other essays

In my eighth decade and other essays

by Alan Bush

Kahn & Averill, London

First published in 1980 by Stanmore Press Ltd
under their associated imprint: Kahn & Averill
Copyright © 1980 by Alan Bush

With grateful acknowledgements to *Frederick Muller
Ltd; The Musical Times* and *Music.*

British Library Cataloguing in Publication Data

Bush, Alan
    In my eighth decade and other essays.
    1. Music — History and criticism
    I. Title
    780'.92'4   ML160
    ISBN 0-900707-61-5

Printed in Great Britain by
REDWOOD BURN LIMITED
Trowbridge & Esher

Contents

1

In my eighth decade

It is more than fifty years since I started to ask myself what the world was about. I am now seventy-nine and I don't expect that the basic conclusions I have come to are likely to change. This is not because my brain is showing any signs of ossification. If I have mellowed — the term often politely applied to the enfeebled views of the elderly — this is because my continuous and varied reading over the last twenty years or so has somewhat altered my sense of perspective, though not in any way my general world-outlook.

In 1934 I became convinced that the facts about life, including human life, and about the inorganic world from stellar galaxies to atoms and for that matter to other particles discovered by 20th century nuclear physics, were convincingly explained or brilliantly foretold between the years 1844 and 1896 by Karl Marx and Friedrich Engels.

Marxism is indeed a potent and invaluable guide to action in politics. But there are problems on which Marx and Engels wrote little, those of art and morals, especially the latter. The problem of personal responsibility faces everyone. Are our deeds inexorably determined by our emotional condition at any given moment, which is itself the result of memories of past experiences and education acting on such brains and glandular secretions as we have inherited and the relatively complete or incomplete functioning of which is dependent upon age, food, sexual situation and many other factors which go to make up our state of health at that particular moment? Or are we in possession of free will, even if we don't appear often to exercise it? It is very difficult for a materialist, as a marxist must certainly be, to find room for free will. An intelligent and philosophically trained marxist with whom I raised this problem replied with the utmost seriousness: "We are both free and unfree." This seemingly dialectical proposition did not tell me very much. I have found the answer, as I believe, in Jean-Paul Sartre's *L'Être et le Néant**, where he gives an explanation of how the structure of human consciousness makes freedom of action (or inaction) not only possible but inescapable. We are therefore doomed to be free. This theory contradicts most of the mutually conflicting pseudo-scientific theories of psychology, fashionable in present-day Britain, but this is proof rather than disproof of its correctness. I find Sartre's argumentation on this point convincing.

As I am a composer and performer of music it is important to me to understand art to the best of my ability. I have found historical materialism the only adequate explanation of the facts of musical history and the only objective method by means of which anybody can hope to arrive at a critical evaluation of any particular work of art.

Marxism explains in broad outline but quite clearly where we are in the historical process and in what direction the next steps forward ought to be taken. If you are so situated that you can be an active participant in a revolutionary action of the working-class, this answers for you the question: "What is the point of living at all?" An individual life is inevitably short in comparison with any historical epoch, though not necessarily brutal, as Hobbes described it. How can you enjoy and therefore love life if you happen by chance to have been born in a country so politically backward as Great Britain has proved itself to be since the end of the Second World War, and if it seems, therefore, that through no fault of your own, frustration is to be your portion as far as the historical process is concerned? Homo sapiens, the species of which I am proud and fortunate to be an individual example, is my exclusive concern, either in other individual examples or as a whole. But what if so considerable a majority of the specimens among whom chance has thrown me by the accident of birth appear at this moment in history to be, from the point of view of social or historical consciousness, more like domestic animals than men and women, or else, though knowledgeable, corrupted by insidious careerist pressures, so that history will pass us all by? How then can I hope to love life, I ask myself?

I ought to explain here that this essay is not meant to be an intimate, self-revealing autobiography. A lot of my time I am occupied

---

*Jean-Paul Sartre: *Being & Nothingness*, p.31. (London: Methuen, 1957.)

unavoidably in sleeping (and therefore dreaming), washing, dressing and undressing, eating, drinking or with other physiological necessities. But to none of this shall I refer, except in so far as any one of them may have influenced me in what I think about the world, or may arouse particular thoughts in my mind. Thus I might mention that I never turn on the bath-tap but that I think of the complex human activities which have been purposefully co-ordinated in order to make this routine act of hygiene possible. There is the past scientific work, which has gone into the mass production of ceramics and complicated metal-work; furthermore there are the present human actions, organised day after day, which are indispensable to the maintenance of the water supply. I never cease to marvel at the intricacy of the social threads which are interwoven in order to make possible these happenings, while at the same time the whole process is taken so much as a matter of course that hardly one man or woman in a thousand gives it a thought, except to moan if something goes wrong.

And then, luckily for me, there is also loving. This is a very strange thing indeed. Even human love shows in some instances undelectable varieties of behaviour; these result from the fact that cultural evolution during the past eight thousand years or so could only develop within the framework of some form or other of class society with its distorting results for the human individual. Indeed such distortions have been inevitable until in 1917 the break-through of the October Revolution ushered in a new era in human history. Furthermore, love in other worlds than ours proceeds at times in unimaginably grotesque fashion. The normal sequence of events in the love-life of the praying mantis must certainly put an end to any notion that love is divine; it is hard to approve from any point of view such complete disregard by the female mantis for the feelings of a passionate swain as to make of him her repast, almost before he has finished yielding up his contribution to the preservation of the species.

Yet love in the insect world has its glories also. Take, for example, the spurge-louse, an insect in whose procreation only about one male in a hundred takes any part. The young males, less than one tenth of an inch long, possess an aigrette of white filaments. "In moments of elation the tip of the abdomen rises between the lifted wings and a bundle of spokes spread out fan-wise. The insect is showing off, erecting his tail like the peacock. To glorify his nuptials he has attached a comet's tail to his rump; he displays it fan-wise, closes it, opens it again, making it quiver and glisten in the sunlight. When the crisis of joy has passed his finery is folded up and the abdomen sinks down under cover of the wings."* The rapturous moment in the life of the young louse is over. Wandering away, he finds a quiet spot to die, not, it is true, as the victim of his partner's gluttony, but because he possesses no stomach, no mouth even; he cannot eat and so cannot remain alive for more than a few hours.

For me love has brought as complete a happiness in life as a man could hope to experience, born as I was in a country of the Western World in its decline. (In a later paragraph the chance which made this happiness possible will receive its due mention.)

The facts of natural history are indeed hardly less improbable than those of human history, from the point of view of the individual man, woman or child, are alarming. Yet ever since life appeared on this planet Earth it has fought a winning battle against death. In this year 1980 a.d. organisms in inexhaustible variety and ever increasing numbers come to birth, live and die; some enjoy a life-span of hours, others of days, weeks, months, years, even of centuries. The vast majority, except for us humans, meet with a fatal accident long before their life has reached maturity, let alone old age; among us millions of men, women and children in the underdeveloped countries are dying of hunger and preventable diseases. Since 1945 in many countries of the world hundreds of thousands have died in murderous wars, initiated by the governments of Britain, China, France, Israel, Pakistan and the United States of America. How can this have happened and what can be done about such a state of affairs?

I am firmly of the opinion that much can be done as far as the human world is concerned. There is no scientific basis for long-term pessimism. An organism with consciousness and the power of reflection and one which has found the way to planned co-operation and creative adaptation to the problems set by life can surely learn to avoid totally unnecessary mutual descructiveness.

But to explain how I have arrived at these opinions I must pass in review the many facets of my education, which began, as it does with everyone who started life with a more or less normal family environment, at home.

I was the youngest of a family of three boys. My father and mother were both members of ample Victorian middle-class families, my father

*Henri Fabre: *The Life of the Scorpion*, pp307/8. (Hodder and Stoughton; London, 1923.)

one of thirteen children, ten of whom grew to maturity, my mother one of six. Both were brought up as conventional Anglican Christians. My father was a complete philistine in religious and philosophical questions; in politics he took no active part, though he always voted conservative in elections. My mother retained vague remembrances of her religious upbringing but never went to church herself, though she required us boys to attend whatever local Anglican house of worship there happened to be nearby. This rule was not so strictly insisted upon by her as to prevent my father from taking us quite often on Sundays to the London Zoo, something which roused in me an interest in the animal kingdom which I have never lost, though I have never much wanted to keep pets. My mother as a girl had shown considerable talent as a graphic artist, but a professional career in this field was considered disreputable by her parents and therefore forbidden. Her proposals to become a doctor or even a hospital nurse were likewise discouraged, the former as outré and in any case very expensive and the latter as unlady-like. So as a last resort she adopted matrimony as her profession and accepted my father's offer. Her immense energy and formidable organising capacity were therefore concentrated on her household and family. Her efforts to organise the less essential details of my life caused some tension at times, but she never interfered in any decisions I took in matters of career, pursuit of education or marriage.

My parents separated legally after 35 years of marriage, during the last 18 of which they had lived somewhat of a tigress and dog life. My father died of cancer in 1934 at the age of 68, my mother of old age in 1950 at 87. The last five years or so of her life were burdened by physical disabilities, so much so that at one point she attempted suicide and was only prevented from succeeding by the skill of her doctor.

Before turning to my personal experiences I must mention one further matter which concerned some members of my father's family and which came to affect me strongly at one stage of my life. Some years after the death of my paternal grandfather in 1888 his widow became involved in spiritualism. One of her daughters-in-law developed mediumistic tendencies, producing in trance conditions both mental and physical phenomena. Following her advice when in trance six members of the family embarked on a voyage round the world in search of valuable hidden treasure, the exact whereabouts of which were to be duly disclosed from the astral plane when the time was ripe. The journey was doubtless beneficial to all the travellers from a cultural point of view. The heavy expense involved did not, however, result in any material profit. The whereabouts of the hidden treasure remained undisclosed and the financial balance sheet showed a heavy loss. I would not mention this bizarre incident in my family history except as evidence of the extreme seriousness with which the advice believed to be that of departed spirits or other denizens of "higher" planes was listened to by some members of my father's family.

In a large family of English people, removed from immediate contact with the processes of production, the gentlemanly eccentric could hardly fail to appear. One of my father's brothers, at first a devout Anglican, turned to spiritualism in a big way, propagating it publicly as a new religion, and with it in his case were associated all the idiosyncracies of the bourgeois or petty-bourgeois humanitarian such as dietary fads, teetotalism and even nudism, which do not involve any practical action for radical social change. This respectable suburban householder had at various times of his life been in the habit of eating coal and taking dew baths naked in his back garden. In another uncle the results were more sensational. For the last forty-five years of his life he became an obsessive student and would-be practitioner of occultism. His library shelves were weighed down with the works of Paracelsus, Eliphas Levi and Madame Blavatsky. He became expert in the drawing of cabbalistic figures on the floor, from within the protection of which he would attempt at an appropriate phase of the sun, moon and planets to call up the spirits of the deep. For this uncle of mine the world was peopled, not only by the plants and other physical organisms which we all know, but also by an innumerable host of so-called elementals, beings possessed of an astral body, which we humans are also believed by occultists to possess; although they are without a physical body and therefore invisible to normal sight, they are inexplicably able to act in some circumstances upon physical matter. To learn to control the elementals was this uncle's ambition. What interest to him the laborious and costly control of nature by scientific technique, when the elementals could be commanded to transport material objects instantaneously from pole to equator or to extract the contents of the most modern safe without recourse to any combination! If possessed of these powers this uncle of mine could, if he so wished, have the crown jewels from the Tower of London deposited before him on his suburban drawing-room carpet. This uncle, a qualified solicitor and competent business executive, twice happily married and father of an upstanding son, was not insane. He did not believe that he possessed such powers. But he did believe that his experiences of mediumistic phenomena justified him in the opinion that it was possible to acquire them. And so he devoted the spare time of his whole adult life to the attempt.

My childhood was happy. My mother was devotedly affectionate, my father invariably kind and attentive. Except during the grouse-shooting season he spent his Sundays with us three boys as a matter of course. The tension between my parents did not become apparent until I was about sixteen years old.

Up to the age of twenty-five I was extremely delicate. I have had in all five surgical operations, the third when I was twenty-five, after which my health became robust. If it had not been my good fortune on account of my parents' wealth to be able to take full advantage of the present state of medical knowledge I should certainly not be alive to-day. I am therefore very enthusiastic about its practice and development. It is one of the most serious crimes of the imperialists, led by United States imperialism, that the expenses of their war preparations so savagely reduce the amounts of money which could otherwise be invested in medical research and hospital treatment.

My parents sent my two elder brothers, Alfred and Brinsley, successively to two private preparatory boarding schools, both highly recommended by the scholastic agencies who earned their profits by touting for pupils. At these establishments Alfred's health was badly neglected while Brinsley was flogged every now and again, I don't know for what misdemeanours, so they were both brought home and for a year or more we were all taught by tutors or governesses. Owing to my delicate health I continued to be taught privately until, at eleven and a half I went as a day-boy to Sir Roger Cholmeley's Grammar School in Highgate, North London and stayed there until Christmas, 1917. I do not remember being particularly happy at school or very unhappy. The headmaster was a mathematician who fostered science, in which my interest was aroused. I proved, however, to be a most unskilful experimenter in the chemistry lab; dangerous acids boiled over and such crude apparatus as we had at our disposal was often irreparably damaged wherever I happened to be working. In 1917 I managed to pass the London Matriculation in both Chemistry and Electricity and Magnetism, as this branch of physics was then called; fortunately for me no practical tests in either subject were required.

I was not getting my musical education at school but privately. My mother, as I mentioned, had studied painting to good effect; she had been taught the piano and singing, which were both considered ladylike accomplishments. My brothers were both put to the piano at an early age. Alfred showed outstanding facility. My father was encouragingly benevolent towards this activity; when Alfred developed quite early the ability to play from memory he earned tips from my father, sixpence for each page of music which he could perform without the copy. My fourth birthday was approaching. My mother asked what I would like for a birthday present. I said: "A piano lesson." So it was arranged that our family teacher, who followed Mrs Curwen's pianoforte method, should pay us a special visit on 22nd December, 1904. Ever since, except for the years 1941-45, which I spent in the British Army, and for most of the subsequent twenty-five years, during which I wrote my four operas and participated in nine of their twelve professional productions, I have been practising the piano off and on under a succession of teachers. The most recent lessons I took were in 1979 with the magnificent pianist and splendid piano teacher Harold Rubens. I showed no talent or facility, but I evidently developed an interest in playing the piano as an occupation from the very start. When six years old I used to spend hours plodding through pages of piano music from my mother's library; this included Hummel and Clementi and also grand fantasias by forgotten composers on such operas as Verdi's *La Traviata* and Gounod's *Faust*. Now I come to think of it, the subject matter of these works was curiously unsuitable for a boy of six, but no one raised this particular problem and in any case I had no idea what the stories of the operas were about. My piano playing was not practising and no doubt helped to form atrocious pianistic habits; but it developed my powers of sight-reading and later, as a student of the Royal Academy of Music, I was perhaps the second-best sight-reader in the building, the uncrowned king of this domain being my fellow-student Reginald Paul.

In August, 1914, the First World War broke out. At its beginning this made very little impact on our family life. Alfred was then too delicate to volunteer and Brinsley too young. My father's economic position improved, war being "terribly profitable", as Lenin was most pertinently to observe, so there was no lack of money.

During the Easter holidays of 1915 or 1916, I do not remember which, something momentous happened to me by chance. I was walking through the streets of Highgate when I noticed a brass plate on a front door, bearing the inscription "Branch of the Hornsey Public

Library." Up to that moment I did not know that such an institution as a public library existed. Full of curiosity, I walked in and was allowed to wander among the shelves. I was amazed to discover that a lot of people had written serious books concerning the problem of what the world was really about in its essence (philosophy) and what human beings had made or were making of their lives (politics). This was the beginning of my general education.

I learnt that for the last two hundred and fifty years or so many philosophers had spent a great deal of their energy discussing how we could prove that what we felt quite sure was true could be known by us to be the truth. At that time it seemed to me that this problem occupied these well-meaning men to the exclusion of more important questions. I could not help wondering why these philosophers had paid so little attention to alleviating the horrors of human life, which were beginning to dawn on me, a mere schoolboy of fifteen. The shelves of the Hornsey Branch Library were not in those days weighed down with the works of Marx, Engels and Lenin. So I did not then find the answer to the question: "what is truth?" nor could I then know that these three thinkers had themselves arrived at their scientifically correct answers by studying the works and developing the ideas while unveiling the inadequacies of their predecessors.

One truly wonderful book which made the greatest impression on me of any that I read at that time was Ernst Haeckel's *Riddle of the Universe.* * His discovery that primitive unicellular organisms possess, albeit in the most elementary form imaginable, the power to register sense impressions from the outside world and to react as a result with pleasure or revulsion, filled me with delight. Following upon this I came upon Darwin's theory of natural selection. This disclosed to me the unified development of the entire animal kingdom, including our own species, homo sapiens. The marvel of consciousness, above all of human consciousness, that wonderful state of existence of matter at its highest molecular complication, filled me with awe. I adopted mechanical materialism as my world outlook. Life became my Pantheon and homo sapiens the object of my devotion. I never doubted that the development of living from inorganic matter would in due course be achieved scientifically in the laboratory. During the last

---

*Ernst Haeckel: *The Riddle of the Universe*, pp 122-124. (London; Thinkers Library, Watts and Co., 1946.)

thirty years the work of J.D. Bernal, Francis Crick and James D. Watson brought this achievement nearer. I recently read the following:

> In 1965, a team at the University of Illinois under Professor Sol Spiegelman in a brilliant series of experiments succeeded in putting together the non-living nucleic-acid message which produced a virus which would go on and multiply indefinitely. Their artificial virus was completely indistinguishable from a natural virus.*

But to return to my out-of-school education, I continued to swim fascinated among the book-islands of the Branch Library and paused before books on sociology. I remember particularly two early works by H.G. Wells, *Anticipations* and *Mankind in the Making*. Christopher Caudwell, to date the greatest British marxist theoretician of art, wrote the following: "Wells is a petit-bourgeois, and of all the products of capitalism none is more unlovely than this class",** and also "The subtlest and acutest hypothesis in his hands somehow becomes clumsy and shoddy. Science's most vital discoveries recounted by him seem grey and linen-draperish."** This condemnation overlooks Well's one positive contribution, that as the populariser of his own particular brand of Utopian socialism, he did disclose many of the vile injustices of capitalism and the hypocrisies of its propagandists. I thus became aware of the fact that human society was not organised in a way which enabled all men and women, the most splendid of nature's products, to live out their lives to the full, either in Britain or elsewhere; on the contrary it was quite evidently geared to promote the material advantage of a small group of rich families and to maintain their power over the poor. To the question of how this had come about Wells provided no answer. To overcome it he proposed that more money should be spent by the state on education, as a result of which a larger number of people would become more knowledgeable and therefore more reasonable and would thus tend to improve the human situation generally, more or less as a matter of course.

As a young person, who had been kindly brought up and armoured against any arrow of poverty within the carapace of a solid economic family position, I might perhaps have found contentment in this mild social Micawberism of H.G. Wells. After all, it is to this day the

---

*G. Rattray Taylor: *The Biological Time Bomb*, p. 203. (London; Panther Books, 1968.)
**Christopher Caudwell: *Studies in a Dying Culture*, pp.76 and 94. (London, The Bodley Head, 1949.)

mental sago-pudding in which millions of rank and file supporters of social democracy in the West continue to flounder, thus providing their leaders and publicists with respectable and well-paid careers under the protection of the imperialist umbrella.

But the crisis of which the First World War was the ghastly symptom broke down the walls of countless bourgeois family strongholds. In 1917 my eldest brother, Alfred, was killed in Flanders in one of the useless blood-baths with which Allied or German generals organised occasional interruptions to the quiet on the Western Front. At this point the above-mentioned peculiarity in my family history came into play. My occultist uncle encouraged my parents to seek consolation in the séance room. For several years table-turning, the ouija-board and mediums in trance transmitted messages, purporting to come from my brother Alfred and from other deceased friends and relations, in some of whom we had little interest. The mediums passed through an intermediate stage in which they showed a change of personality; at such times they were "controlled by their spirit guides" and often spoke some odd kind of broken English. After this introductory period they would pass into a deeper trance and we were addressed by a different personality who introduced itself as that of our departed brother; he had survived the destruction of his material body and was living on in some etheric world, which interpenetrated with our physical one. Looking back on these time-consuming evenings, I cannot recall that the personalities of those who had "passed over" conveyed any profound understanding of the problems of life or gave us any helpful advice. They told us to be cheerful, not to mourn their loss unduly, since everything was quite nice in their particular region of the astral plane, rather as it used to be on earth on a quiet Sunday afternoon — no work to do, of course — though no doubt there might in other spheres be horrors which they personally had not deserved and also raptures which they had not as yet earned.

I soon learnt that spiritualism was a rather limited and low-grade department in the wider field of occultism, and that the latter had achieved a kind of pseudo-scientific respectability within the world-outlook of theosophy. I deserted for the time being the Hornsey Branch Library for the incense- and guru-haunted premises of the Theosophical Society, of which I was a member for several years. I was quickly introduced to the theory of incarnation. This is the most demoralising of all religious beliefs. It teaches that we are all born into the material and hereditary conditions to which our actions in past lives entitle us. To the under-privileged it counsels resignation, with the consolation that he or she is working out past sins and thus earning a better future in the next life on earth. To a person fortunately circumstanced by birth, as I was, it is an inducement to complacency and renders the chance misfortunes of others matters almost of indifference, since they are all justly measured in the scales and meted out by Karma, the Hindu word for fate. The inescapable mould of each individual's character and future prospects, which have been accumulated from countless past lives, can be disclosed by the study of astrology, which has been recently described by Professor Farrington as "the most devastating, the most crippling of all superstititions."* It should give us pause when we realise that here in Britain in the late 20th century several of our popular newspapers devote inches of type-space every day to this pre-Christian hangover. I blush to recall that at that time of my life I cast my own horoscope and those of a few other people round me.

The aim of the theosophist is to arrive at the status of adept or mahatma, when the wheel of Karma ceases for him or her to turn; the guru is someone on the lower slopes of this Himalayan elevation. I learnt that to achieve this condition I would have to submit to long years, probably many lives of self-abnegating discipline, and that the "truth of the way" would be disclosed to me at various stages of the path by more spiritually advanced persons placed in authority over me. I could not find the "truth" out for myself; I could not know for myself that it was the "truth", but must accept it as such on somebody else's authority.

Once I realised that this was so, the whole tuppence - coloured balloon collapsed. I determined to try and find out what I was in a position to know for myself about the world and about man, without having to accept anything on the authority of another person. We must each of us live, I said to myself, according to what we can know, even if it isn't very much. And I realised that I did not then know how much or how little it would prove to be.

From 1915 onwards I began to compose short pieces, some of which pleased while others aggrieved my teacher of that time, William Wooding Starmer, a devoted musician whose chief interest was in campanology. His life-long hope was to see carillons, like those of Belgium, gracing all British cathedrals, from whose towers virtuoso

*Farrington: *The Faith of Epicurus*, p.74. (London; Weidenfeld & Nicholson, 1967.)

carillonneurs would daily transmit in bell tones folk and classical melodies. This idea, if put into practice, would certainly provide better public fare than the sound-saccharine of today's supermarkets and railway cafeterias.

My constant and developing musical activity decided me to devote my life to music instead of to industrial science, to which my father's business connections would otherwise have led me. I entered the Royal Academy of Music as a student in January, 1918, remaining there until July, 1922; I studied composition with Frederick Corder, piano with Tobias Matthay and organ with Reginald Steggall. After this I continued my studies privately until 1927 in composition with John Ireland and in piano with Benno Moiseiwitsch and his assistant, Mabel Lander, and for the year 1928 in piano with Artur Schnabel.

While a student at the R.A.M. it so happened that a young composer, Michael Head, won a composition scholarship and entered Frederick Corder's class. We became friends and in 1921 I visited his home and came to know his younger sister Nancy. She became my wife in 1931 and our life together has brought days, months, years, indeed decades of ever deepening happiness in uninterrupted succession. Besides this it was my rare good fortune that in my wife I found the librettist of three of my four full-length operas, three childrens' operas and numerous other vocal works.

During the four years I spent at the R.A.M. I paid little attention to world affairs. This is to be accounted for by my studies on the one hand and on the other that I was still edging my way along the seven-fold path of theosophy without having reached the empty centre of the maze.

It is true that the October Revolution had taken place. But I had fallen a victim to the enraged screams of the Allied Governments at the treachery of Lenin in signing a separate peace with the Germans. As late as 1936 Professor H.A.L. Fisher, the greatest pundit among the Oxford historians, described Lenin as "an adventurer" and "of an almost unequalled capacity for making himself disagreeable"*; the fact that a revolution in Britain was avoided in the early 19th century was attributed by Professor Fisher to "the kind providence which has presided over English politics, furnishing the best Tory leaders with a measure of pliability and good sense."** Such fatuity on the part of

*H.A.L. Fisher: *A History of Europe*, Vol II, p.1243 (London: Fontana Library, 1969.)
** Ibid: pages 986/7.

leading intellectuals of the British Establishment does not, however, prevent their poison from having an influence, especially among young middle-class intellectuals, of which I was one.

After I finished my studies at the R.A.M., where music was music and life was life and never the twain seemed to meet, I discovered that there were in existence organisations of working-class people whose aim was the establishment of the rational society of socialism. I became aware that a socialist state had been set up in the Union of Soviet Socialist Republics. In 1924 I joined the Independent Labour Party, at that time the socialist wing of the Labour Party, and a year later I became an active member of the London Labour Choral Union, whose aim was to promote the cause of socialism through musical activity; it was led by the famous English composer Rutland Boughton. I wrote songs for this organisation. Moreover I began to take part in general working-class activities such as parliamentary elections as a canvasser and later the hunger-marches. In 1929 the I.L.P., influenced by Trotskyism, disaffiliated from the Labour Party, so I resigned from it and joined the Labour Party.

By this time I had realised that I must learn more about the world, more about politics. To this end I entered Berlin University as a student in 1929 and started on the systematic study of philosophy with musicology as my second subject. In due course I came into contact with the works of Marx, Engels and Lenin and with the music of composers associated with the German working-class movement, such as Hanns Eisler, whose world-outlook was that of marxism. Economic problems, my marriage and the threatening rise of Hitler fascism in Germany decided me to return to England in the summer of 1931 after only two-and-a-half years as a student in Berlin University. Already thirty years old, I abandoned any attempt to take a D.Phil. in Berlin, which would have taken nearly three more years.

My studies and my experiences in Berlin in the early 30s, the world economic crisis, the failure of social democracy in the Weimar Republic to prevent the seizure of power by German fascism, the high culture and heroism of the communist workers of Germany — it took all this to bring me from the mechanical materialism of my boyhood to marxism, the world-outlook I adopted in 1934. I joined the Communist Party of Great Britain in 1935.

For me, as a musician and as a man, marxism is a guide to action. It challenges me to express through musical art the feelings of men and women, above all in their struggles to create a condition of social organisation in which science and art will be the possession of all and in which they will themselves be no longer exploiters nor objects of exploitation.

Among those of my compositions in which this challenge has been most clearly taken up are my four full-length operas, one of them a prize-winner in the Arts Council Opera Competition of 1951. It has been my inestimable good fortune to see them all produced in seven different opera houses of the German Democratic Republic as well as one in a London opera house and another one in two opera houses of the U.S.S.R.

The first step along the road which led to my fruitful and happy association with the Leipzig Opera House was taken in Berlin in 1931, when I entered the Grosses Schauspielhaus to hear the first performance of *Die Massnahme,* a Lehrstueck by Bertolt Brecht with music by Hanns Eisler. Three years later in London I met the composer with two of his former students and fellow fighters with him for working-class power, Ernst Hermann Meyer and Georg Knepler. All four of us were active musically in the British working-class movement; songs by Eisler and Meyer became famous in Britain and in 1934/35 I conducted in different districts in London ten performances of *Die Massnahme* in an English translation.

As an English citizen who has fought for socialism I owe much, very much, probably my life to the glorious Red Army; as a composer the opera houses of the German socialist state have provided me with the opportunities and therefore the instigation to create the three full-length operas which have succeeded my first opera: *Wat Tyler.*

For I did not write *Wat Tyler* with either Leipzig or the G.D.R. in mind. An English Marxist historian, Hyman Fagan, had suggested the English peasant rising of 1381 as a good subject for an opera as early as 1938. During the time I was serving with the British Army, my wife Nancy and I visited Maidstone, where John Ball, one of the leaders of the rebellion, was freed from imprisonment in Maidstone Gaol, a mediaeval fortress which is still standing. Nancy wrote the libretto in 1947 and I started to compose the music in 1948. In 1951 the Verband Deutscher Komponisten and Musikwissenschaftler invited me to their inaugural conference; I asked my friends, Eisler, Meyer and Knepler to arrange an occasion on which I could sing and play it through to possibly interested people. At that meeting those present included the composer Rudolf Wagner-Regeny, and Hans Pischner, then music director of the Berliner Rundfunk. Dr. Pischner, as he then was, at once decided to record an extensive radio version of *Wat Tyler* in German translation, which I conducted early in 1952 with singers from all over the G.D.R. and choir and symphony orchestra of the Berliner Rundfunk. A decision to produce the opera in the Leipzig Opera House in May, 1953, was quickly taken and I went home to England after the most exciting period of my professional life.

The world premiere of *Wat Tyler* took place in September of 1953. I spent 14 days before the premiere in Leipzig and my practical education as an opera composer began. The opera then consisted of an orchestral prelude, a prologue, Act I with three scenes, Act II with two scenes and an epilogue. There would be two pauses, one after Act I, scene 3, the second after Act II, scene 2. The producer, Mr. Voigt, proposed that the Epilogue should be added to Act II as a third scene; a pause after Act II, scene 2 in which the hero, Wat Tyler, meets his death would be disastrous, he argued. He was right. This change necessitated composing an orchestral interlude about three and a half minutes long to accompany the change of scene between the second and third scenes of Act II.

The success of the première of *Wat Tyler* was an exceedingly important event in my life, not only because it put me on the map as an opera composer but because it introduced me to Karl Kayser, who was present at the performance and at the reception afterwards.

My wife and I wrote our second opera, *Men of Blackmoor*, with a first performance in the G.D.R. in view. A proposal to produce the opera in Weimar in November, 1956, was made by Karl Kayser, then the intendant there. I tried to persuade Karl Kayser to produce *Men of Blackmoor* with myself at his elbow on the musical side, and he agreed. Other commitments intervened, however, and eventually it was decided that I should produce it with his general advice and detailed assistance. This arrangement worked out well, and the three months I spent in Weimar in the autumn of 1956 were the happiest of my professional life, though not of my personal life, because my wife had to remain in England for various reasons and only came over for the premiere.

Shortly after the premiere of *Men of Blackmoor* I returned to England, but not before Karl Kayser had expressed an interest in the idea of my writing a third opera. I eagerly seized upon this and my first journey to collect material in British Guyana for an opera about the struggle of the Guyanese people in 1953 against British imperialism took place in the summer of 1957. I was, however, forbidden to land in the colony by the authorities, and it took many months to get the ban withdrawn so that I finally made the journey in 1959.

In 1958 in Weimer I met Hans Sachs, the radio representative with whom I became closely associated artistically, as it was he who brought me the invitation of the Radio G.D.R. to compose a substantial orchestral work, the *Byron Symphony* being the result. The first performance of this work with the choir and symphony orchestra of the Leipzig Radio, conducted by Herbert Kegel, was repeated during the Handel Festival at Halle in June and I was honoured later in the same year by the award of a Handel prize from the city of Halle.

In the meantime I had been working on the third opera, *The Sugar Reapers*, or *Guyana Johnny*, to give it it's German title. The world premiere took place in December, 1956, when the audience included a party from Britain, guests of the opera house and of the Leipzig Friends of Britain. Sir Thomas Armstrong, principal of the Royal Academy of Music, London, also undertook the journey.

The devotion to the work which had been shown by the conductor, Rolf Reuter, from the very start of the discussions, the understanding and sympathetic approach of the producer Mr. Fritz Bennewitz and the enthusiasm of the solo and choir singers for their parts made a deep impression on me.

As in the case of *Men of Blackmoor* the Radio of the G.D.R. recorded an extensive radio version of the opera, so that the magnificent interpretation of the Leipzig Ensemble with the Gewandhaus orchestra now exists in a tape-recording.

Guyana Johnny constitutes the third and last paragraph in the first chapter of my opera composing; in these three works the struggle of peasants, industrial workers and colonially oppressed people against the ruling class at different periods in the history of my country are given operatic form. I then wrote my fourth opera, *Joe Hill: The Man Who Never Died*, to a libretto by the American playwright, Barrie Stavis which was produced at the Deutsche Staatsoper, Berlin in September 1970.

In recalling all that I have just related of my artistic life since 1952, it is no wonder that I personally rejoice in the foundation of the German Democratic Republic.

It remains for me to relate some facts of my personal life and some general experiences of my more recent years before, in conclusion, I express my beliefs and hopes for the nineteen-eighties. Nancy and I had a family of three daughters. To one of them a tragic chance befell; at seven years old she suffered sudden death in a street accident. The passing of thirty-six years has not effaced, has hardly dimmed the remembrance of this cruel disaster. Our two other daughters, our sons-in-law and our seven grandchildren have all greatly enriched our lives.

I have had an unusually adventurous life for a professional musician. I have been imprisoned twice, the first time illegally by the authorities of the U.S.A., the second time mistakenly by those of my own country. In 1936 I participated in a working-class demonstration against Mosley fascism in East London; I found myself being charged by mounted police, the horrific surprise of which cannot be known except by personal experience. I have visited many countries including India under the British Raj. There in 1933 I enjoyed the hospitality of the Anglican Archbishop of India, known as the Metropolitan of India, in his palace in Calcutta. One evening after work I wandered through the streets and a hundred yards or so from the palace I turned by chance down a side-street, where I saw a number of men, women and children lying on the pavement, waiting to die of starvation, when their corpses would be duly removed by the sanitary authorities. This made an impression on me which I have never forgotten. The young chaplains who attended on the Metropolitan in the palace seemed to feel that it was a regretable state of affairs, but evidently providential in some way which we, in our human insufficiency, are unable to fathom.

I have visited the U.S.S.R. eleven times since 1938 and have worked in the opera houses of Tartu and Odessa, during rehearsals of my opera *The Sugar Reapers.* I have visited all the socialist countries of Europe except Albania.

The October Revolution of 1917, the firm establishment first of the U.S.S.R. and then of a group of socialist states in Eastern Europe, all growing steadily richer and more powerful, the continued survival of socialist Cuba despite the grave obstacles put in its way by the United States and the beginnings of socialism in several African states, all these marvels achieved in less than the eight decades of my lifetime so far! This is indeed a matter for rejoicing.

It is true that in the governments of the Western World, headed by that of the United States of America and for the last twenty years joined by the government circles of the Chinese People's Republic, there is still a hope that this wonderful future may be blotted out, as a last resort by the unleashing of a third world war, if necessary a nuclear war, however suicidal its results. Only resolute action by the peoples of these countries can avert these projected crimes.

Yet in any case one certainty remains. Homo sapiens, the beauty of the world, the paragon of animals as Shakespeare described us through the mouth of Hamlet, will not become extinct in a world war, even in a nuclear war. In some habitable territory, perhaps in Africa, perhaps in South America, led, it may be, from Siberia, men and women will build new and glorious socialist states, but under difficulties which our unconquerable species need never have encountered.

Radlett, Herts
May 1980

2

Marxism and music

Of all the arts music is the one which seems farthest removed from the influence of social and economic conditions. Its abstract character appears to lend weight to the supposition that its development has proceeded independently from the rest of man's historical progress. Yet it can be shown incontrovertibly that the various main periods of music coincide with well-marked social and economic changes. The coincidence is often very close. Detailed variations in the form taken by some one particular development in different countries can be attributed to an earlier or later rise to power of a new social class in those countries and to no other cause.

The early predominance of choral over instrumental music, the later emergence of a more individual style of expression culminating in solo singing, finally the growing importance of instrumental music and of concert as opposed to chamber music, are all features in musical history whose appearance at the particular moment when they did appear is only explicable when considered in relation to social and economic conditions. Further, the present anarchy in musical theory and practice, the bewilderment and hostility of audiences when faced with the works of the leading composers of the present day, the complete divorce between 'serious' and 'light' music and the ever-growing proportion of the latter together with its increasing inanity, these are only comprehensible when seen as the counterparts in the musical world of the conflicts and contradictions which beset the capitalist system as it staggers from one crisis to the next.

At different times music's function in society has changed. Starting among primitive peoples as a part of the religious cult, it was used by the Greeks as a scientific and highly rationalised means of producing certain psycho-physiological effects; melodies written in the various scales were supposed to have the effect of inducing different conditions of the mind and soul. In early Christian times the free and improvisatorial style of Gregorian plain-song gave the necessary form through which emotional ecstasy and enthusiasm could be aroused; by the urgency of its desire the soul could be raised to hitherto unknown heights of rapture and holiness. As the growing conflicts within the feudal system made themselves felt, the Church having established itself firmly as the supporter of the feudal land-owners, the function of Church music was to aid in preserving the Church's authority rather than to arouse fervour and creative effort. The Organa of the Notre Dame School, lengthy overpowering compositions based upon the foundation of holy writ and papally sanctified musical themes, performed this function admirably; while the motets which combined together Gregorian melodies, troubadour love-songs and ribald pothouse ditties, mirrored in a striking fashion the gathering crisis within the feudal system.

Popular music, both secular and semi-religious, had always existed alongside the official 'art music' of the various periods. In times of change some of the features of such popular music were incorporated in the new official style. As a rising class made itself felt more and more in the social structure its forms of cultural expression began to influence to a greater and greater extent the predominant art works of the particular age. In addition to this, new requirements developed. Music was needed more and more for home consumption in the houses of the burghers and mercantilists. This new music, the *Ars Nova,* broke through first in fourteenth-century Italy, where the mercantile and early industrial developments were first to appear. The function of this new music was to underline the increased emphasis on individuality and enterprise which led in the religious sphere to the Reformation. Despite the geographical proximity of Italy and France, in the latter country, where the mercantile developments impinged much less strongly upon the feudal system, the *Ars Nova* never contained such progressive features as in Italy; it remained content to preserve many more of the features of the *Ars Antiqua* and to develop much less that was new.

As the mercantile and industrial developments affected human life more and more there resulted an ever rapidly increasing tempo with consequent nervous strain for all. A further problem was set the artist, that of providing for the cultured classes a form of recreation which would absorb the mind and excite or soothe the emotions, a spiritual narcotic, free apparently from the moral objections which can be raised against medicinal drugs when used for pleasurable purposes. Painting, whether religious or secular, remained in virtue of its representational character too clear a reminder of the outside world to provide what was demanded. But instrumental music answered the requirements exactly. Its abstract character provided the means through which the mind could be wafted into a condition where for the time being the consciousness of the material world was obliterated; it could almost provide a substitute for religious consolation, which the growing scientific understanding of mankind was making ever less and less securely grounded.

This function of music as a means of producing mental and emotional effects for all who wanted them turned music into a purchasable commodity. The habit of passively listening to music as opposed to taking part in it developed during the seventeenth and eighteenth centuries. And this concert performance of music modified profoundly the structure of the music itself. No other explanation can be given for the fundamental differences in form and style between the instrumental works of contemporary composers of the seventeenth century, such as Weckmann and Rosenmueller, except the fact that the former wrote for amateur performance at home, whereas the latter had in view performance before an audience which demanded mental and emotional stimulus and satisfaction.

From the sixteenth century onwards the art music of any age has always been of two types. There was one type of music which supported more or less consciously the interests of the ruling classes of the period, either in the form of religious works of the Reformation and counter-Reformation, and the later Protestant Church music and religious oratorios of Germany and England, or in the form of secular vocal works, operas such as Lully wrote for Louis XIV to glorify the absolute monarchy, or in a less obvious way the classical Italian and German operas of the seventeenth and early eighteenth centuries. Alongside this propaganda music there was the so-called 'pure' or abstract instrumental music whose function it was to provide an avenue of escape from reality. A comparison between the works of Bach and Handel viewed in this light is instructive. Their religious works are in the main intended for Protestant churches. Yet their character is very different. Those of Bach, the representative of the German Protestants whose economic expansion was seriously hampered by the political conditions under which they lived, show resignation if not plaintiveness regarding the affairs of this world. Bach's pessimism and longing for death are incomprehensible in a person of his character and abilities except when seen as a reflection in the religious sphere of the dissatisfaction with its material conditions of the class to which he belonged, the German middle class. On the contrary in Handel we see a boundless optimism. Coming into contact with Hamburg, always a flourishing commercial city, later with prosperous Italy, and finally with the ruling classes of England at a time of vigorous expansion in manufacture and trade, Handel's world outlook was naturally cheerful, and he poured into his religious works his confidence in the excellence of the concrete world which he knew. It is in their purely instrumental music that the two composers resemble one another most nearly, and here the function of both was the same, namely, to provide that mental and emotional recreation which the times required.

The popular music of this period consists on the one hand of the pastoral, lyrical, and revolutionary folk-songs of the various countries; folk-songs of the last type are usually omitted from the more reputable collections, but there is, for example, a famous song from the sixteenth century deriving from the German peasant revolution which Luther had opposed so vigorously, and there are no doubt songs of the Diggers and Levellers whose movement was brutally repressed by Cromwell. Very little research in this direction has been yet carried out, however. On the other hand there are the popular operas, of which the *Beggar's Opera* is the most famous, in which criticism of prevailing conditions is often outspoken or implied.

In Josef Haydn we find the only major composer whose output is mainly recreation music. Entering early into the service of an immensely rich Hungarian landowner, his main preoccupation was to provide his employer with a constant stream of instrumental works, and these he produced under ideal conditions, an excellent orchestra being constantly at his disposal. It is natural in these circumstances that, sheltered as he was by his patron from the social and economic upheavals of the time and inclined by his Catholic upbringing to a conservative attitude of mind, problems of instrumental technique and abstract musical form should have absorbed him almost entirely. Yet the influence of outside forces is clearly visible in the direction which his musical development took, following as it did the methods of the Mannheim and Vienna Schools of the early eighteenth century, with their instrumental style devised for concert performance.

The political upheavals of the latter part of the eighteenth century, of which Josef Haydn remained seemingly oblivious, were, on the contrary, a vivid part of the artistic consciousness of both Mozart and Beethoven. Their operas and major vocal works are in many cases directly related to the social conditions in which they found themselves. Both composers identified themselves with the forces of progress against the reactionary feudal influences. In the *Marriage of Figaro* Mozart takes sides with the barber against the aristocrat, and in *Don Giovanni* and the *Magic Flute* he attacks organised religion. The events of his life show that his personal preferences and friendships lay with the commercial classes and not with the aristocracy, whose favours he only sought out of necessity. Beethoven, openly associating himself with the ideals of the French Revolution, though not with its later outcome, espoused in *Fidelio* the cause of freedom, and in the later years of his life in the Ninth Symphony affirmed his belief in the realisation of the ideals of brotherhood among men. His peculiar setting of the *Dona nobis pacem*, with its unexpected passages of threatening trumpet and drum, shows unmistakably that his anxiety was to warn mankind against the material dangers of earthly warfare. Not peace for the soul, either before or after death, but peace among the peoples of the world was his concern.

Thus the highest point in the development of music up to now was reached when it seemed as though there was ground for believing in the gradual amelioration of mankind which the Industrial Revolution appeared to be ushering in. In these Beethoven works we see for the last time music sincerely trying to unite the warring classes of society, in the belief — which was then justifiable — that by this means a new and happy era could be brought in. The gradual disillusionment which followed is mirrored in the increasing romanticism and pessimism of nineteenth-century art. Unable to contemplate the awful degradation of the many for the enrichment of the few which the capitalist system brought about, composers turned their attention more and more away from life. This is most clearly seen in the case of Berlioz, whose life coincided with the earliest stages of French capitalist expansion. Already we find a fantastic romanticism distorting an imagination unsurpassed since in intensity, his only realistic works being frankly militarist in character. Composers tended more and more to seek their inspiration in the sagas of earlier times, in the raptures of personal salvation through love, and finally as the ravages of imperialism made themselves more and more evident in the escape into climes as yet partially unspoilt, as with Debussy and his Spanish and South Sea Island tone poems, and Stravinsky with his phallic Russian Peasant scenes in the *Sacre du Printemps*. A different avenue of escape was in the expression of the personal-psychological reactions of the composer, his soul's sensibilities and miseries being treated as though they were all important in complete disregard of the widespread destitution and physical need of the exploited masses of the world. As an example of this Schoenberg's opera *Erwartung* may be cited, in which an orchestra and solo singer take half an hour to express half a minute's mental and emotional experience in the consciousness of a woman awaiting the advent of her lover.

The present position is a very difficult one. The rising class of the present age, the working class, can only develop its cultural life with extreme difficulty. The atmosphere of the worker's daily work, where the economic suicide of his class goes on without cessation, is no basis for culture. His leisure hours are spent amid the cultural influences of the capitalist state, whose function it is to preserve the present property relations intact as far as possible and whose prime need must therefore be to keep the worker ignorant of his true position and to delude him into thinking that his interests are being served by the preservation of those property relations. Deceit can never form the basis of a living art. Hence it is no wonder that the cultural products of the present ruling classes are so perverse when they are not entirely devoid of any kind of value.

The answer to the problem is to be sought in the discovery of those elements in the worker's life which are peculiar to him as a member of the rising class. These are his consciousness of his position in capitalist society, and his determination to act in order to bring about a classless society in which the property relations will be appropriate to socialised means of production, in which mankind will produce for use and not for individual profit. The worker's culture can only be centred in the class struggle. Out of the experiences and needs of the class struggle will be evolved those new elements which will bring about a true revival of art. At first such works of art, designed as weapons in the class struggle, may be crude and primitive. But they will share these characteristics with the Early Christian music, the early Protestant music and the early expressionist music of the beginning of the seventeenth century when compared with the highly cultivated Greek music, Roman Catholic music, and classical style of the respective periods.

3

Problems of opera

"Music began with singing." Curt Sachs* sums up in this sentence
the results of a lifetime of research into the music of primitive tribal
society. This early music-making was practised by primitive man with
an unbounded enthusiasm and devotion. To him it was no part-time
hobby for leisure hours. It organised the activities and moulded the
feelings of all members of the tribe and thus united them against their
enemies, the weather and the fierce animals whose prey they were. The
dramas of their songs and dances were literally matters of life and
death, intimately bound up with the experiences and actions of their
struggle for existence.

Folk-songs and especially work-songs, such as shanties and reaping or
spinning songs, have preserved through the ages something of the
immediacy of this basic tribal music. Nowadays, as far as our
professional musical world is concerned, it is in opera that its nearest
equivalent is to be found. In opera we experience again the force of
music wedded to human action. In the course of an opera there are
always passages of music which are contemplative, which sum up at
some important situation the feelings of the persons involved in the
events of the story; and often these are the most important musical
moments of the work. But these passages all derive their significance
ultimately from the experiences of the men and women whose actions
constitute the drama.

It has been suggested from time to time by some aestheticians of
music that opera is inferior to various other forms of music, especially

*Curt Sacks: *The Rise of Music in the Ancient World*, (Dent, London).

to symphonic instrumental music or chamber music, precisely because, in opera, music is wedded to words and, still worse, directly or indirectly wedded to action. This theory of the inferiority of opera as a form disregards the physiological, social and historical conditions which lie at the root of the development of music and have given to it most of its ineradicable characteristics; in place of these facts the theory bases itself upon the unconscious prejudices of its protagonists. It cannot therefore be seriously considered.

But to resume: it is evident that opera is the form of music nearest to the fundamentals of the art. The fact that it is the most widely popular form, wherever it has been made available, may very well result from this.

Opera is, however, undoubtedly one of the most difficult forms of music from the composer's point of view. This opinion can be safely inferred, I think, from the fact that there are many fewer masterpieces among operas than among symphonic and choral works, let alone chamber music and solo compositions. The vast repertoire of opera of the last two hundred and fifty years has included probably less than thirty really great works. Of these about half are to be found among the works of four composers, Mozart, Verdi, Wagner and Puccini. Of the remainder, Glinka, Smetana and Tchaikovsky have each contributed several, and Beethoven, Bizet, Gounod, Moussorgsky, Debussy, and Mascagni single examples. (Such operas as *Salome*, *Wozzeck*, *Peter Grimes* and *The Consul*, at present so much admired, await as yet the judgement of posterity.) Compared with the numerous choral and instrumental masterpieces from Bach and Handel to Vaughan Williams and Sibelius this is a very small number.

The composition of an opera presents serious artistic problems. The many diverse factors make unity hard to achieve. Complete lack of unity in the treatment of the text has been accepted in operas such as the *Magic Flute* and *Fidelio*, where the composers allowed spoken dialogue; and an only slightly less drastic disregard of unity has been accepted where the so-called *recitativo secco*, literally "dry recitation", is used. Mozart's recitativo secco is undisguisedly less interesting and significant musically than the main songs and ensembles and also than the orchestral interludes; it is merely a means of rendering musical the declamation of dialogue which cannot be omitted without making the plot unintelligible. Thus in opera Mozart accepts the convention of an alternation of musically significant and musically negligible passages; this he avoids in a symphonic composition, where the linking passages have always some musical significance and are related to the more important passages by key and sometimes also thematically. Of course, in spoken dialogue and recitative the verbal content is significant, but this does not discount the lack of unity in the musical treatment as a whole.

Opera composers have aimed at a solution in various ways. Wagner and Puccini do without recitativo secco. In Wagner the recitative is supported by a dramatically significant orchestral foundation. Puccini sets even the slightest conversational passages to a melodious declamation, carrying more vocal effect than in Mozart's recitativo secco; moreover, his librettist contrives to manage with very few and brief verbal explanations of plot. Verdi in his early operas uses a more expressive recitative than Mozart's recitativo secco, but his songs and ensembles are linked together by relatively insignificant passages; in his later works he employs a melodious cantilena, of which Puccini's musical small talk is the rather characterless echo. This difficult problem is one for the librettist in the first place. It seems to me that small talk, explanation of plot and, above all, narration should be reduced to a minimum and eliminated altogether where possible. The text in the ideal libretto should comprise only the expression of the thoughts and feelings of the characters essential to the particular moment of the action.

But there is a further problem of a different kind. The stage action can easily work against the special characteristics of musical structure. The libretti of operas are nearly always adaptations from already existing stories. The sequences of events can hardly be expected to follow lines of development necessarily well suited to large musical forms. Each act or scene tends, therefore, to resolve itself into a succession of independent sections, each different from the last, and producing as a whole an episodic effect from a musical point of view. Most opera composers from the mid-nineteenth century onwards have aimed at continous music throughout each act; the solo songs, duets and ensembles are all linked together, in many cases the harmonic closes at the end of the various musical sections leading without a break immediately into what follows. But this continuity is often achieved by the disregard of musical structure. The exigencies of stage action are deemed to excuse a musical formlessness, which, in a piece of instrumental music, would result in a lack of intelligibility. The music in such cases is not self-sufficient apart from the stage action; it is lacking in some of the characteristics which are indispensable to a balanced musical form.

Wagner has solved this problem, but at what a cost! He achieves musical structure and continuity by means of a symphonic orchestral foundation which is the battle-ground of the dramatic conflict, which expounds the argument at the rare moments of stage action, and which provides illustration and commentary to the encyclopaedic narrations. In the process he reduces his stage figures for most of the time to declamatory dummies. Except where they are actually singing the leit-motiv melodies in unison with the orchestra, their vocal outlines, though perfectly adapted to the metrical details and meaning of the text, are characterless and undelineated; it is impossible to tell from the musical aspects of their vocal parts whether it is Venus or Fricka, Telramund or Siegmund who is speaking. Continuity and musical structure at the expense of characterisation is not, I believe, the correct solution.

Mozart, in my opinion, has pointed the way. Take, for example, the Trio between the Count, Basilio and Susanna in the first act of *The Marriage of Figaro*. During this passage of music there is a good deal of stage action; Susanna pretends to faint and recovers, the Count discloses Cherubino lying in the chair. Yet the musical construction is so built that the stage action moulds it without rendering it formless. Besides this, the vocal lines of the three characters are clearly differentiated, each fitting the expression by the particular person of his or her feelings at the moment. The second act of *Fidelio* is a comparable masterpiece of musical form and character delineation.

These various problems were uppermost in my mind while I was working on my opera *Wat Tyler*. It was my unique good fortune to find in my own wife a librettist with whom many basic difficulties could be faced. In her libretto explanation and narrative are reduced to a minimum, occupying less than ten minutes in a whole of more than two and a half hours. In order to reconcile and satisfy the rival claims of musical requirement and realistic development of the story, there are a number of set pieces in the shape of solo songs, but these only occur where, in the actual circumstances of the time, the persons concerned might in reality have broken into song or found themselves plunged in meditation.

The Prologue, Acts 1 and 2, and the Epilogue are each set as a continuous piece of music, in which are to be found solo songs, duets, ensembles, choruses, music accompanying stage action and the few passages of informative dialogue and explanation. I have aimed at achieving a coherent musical structure in each of these four continuous passages of music, two of which are an hour or more in length. Each scene possesses what may be described as an introduction and coda, while the central portion includes main sections, bridge passages and developments. The orchestra is not, however, the battle-ground; the persons on the stage bear both the dramatic and musical burden, the orchestra being designed as a support, or, if you like, an accompaniment to their singing and acting. Only during the changes between the scenes of Acts 1 and 2, when the curtain is down, the orchestra must needs occupy the whole musical canvas; and in Act 2 there is an orchestral interlude, "The Peasant Army at Blackheath", which represents the elation of the peasants on reaching London, their arrival being the only event essential to the story which is not enacted on the stage.

I have made deliberate efforts to delineate the characters throughout in their actual vocal lines. Thanks to the almost complete avoidance of small talk, the characters have only things to say which advance the story and set forth their part in it. They are thus themselves in every word they sing and can be individually treated musically without interfering with a convincing effect. It would be difficult to arrange for two characters to say "Oh, what a beautiful morning" with an individually distinct vocal intonation and to make the two passages sound equally convincing. But significant dialogue can display in every detail the characteristics of the person concerned. This process of characterisation is underlined by the orchestra, but it is centred in the utterances of the persons themselve¯

Space and the absence of musical examples prevent me from explaining how I set about this process of characterisation by vocal intonation. There is, of course, nothing new about it as a feature of opera. Mozart, Beethoven, Glinka, Bizet, Tchaikovsky and Moussorgsky have all made it one aspect of their operatic method. But they have not always carried it out consistently, as it seems to me. The exigencies of musical form have sometimes, even with Mozart, taken precedence over individual characterisation. In *Wat Tyler* I have aimed at consistency in this respect and have abandoned it only at one place, the ensemble which ends Act 2, where John Ball, the Herdsman and the Escaped Serf join with a group of the peasant army men in a lament over the hero's body after his murder by the nobles; here I have allowed the unity of feeling between them all to over-ride the individuality of these three characters, and their ensemble becomes a kind of stanzic song with coda, in which the verses, allotted to different persons, are all set to one developing and even recurrent melody.

It is with great interest that I await the opinion of the musical public on *Wat Tyler*. The first production will take place at the Municipal Opera House, Leipzig, next April, in a German translation. I hope after this to enjoy the opportunity of seeing it produced in its original language and performed to my countrymen, for whom it was primarily written.

4

On the study and teaching of musical composition

Musical composition has been learned and taught in Western Europe for about a thousand years. For the first one hundred and fifty years of this time the musical treatises covered the whole subject of music and did no more, as far as composition was concerned, than expound the methods whereby countermelodies to the Plainchants were being improvised by singers. But in the *Musica* of John Cotton, dated approximately 1100, we have a genuine treatise on composition. In this work the author lays down general principles and gives practical examples which are designed to show that alternative solutions to a particular problem are possible; one melody is taken and various contermelodies provided by the author.

From that date until quite recent times (say the year 1920, which, however, varied from one country to another) these two aspects of the teaching of composition have always been considered necessary; there has always been an accepted system of general principles and, in addition, practical exercises have been provided by means of which the student learns to apply these principles as he considers best.

These general principles have, of course, changed as music has developed. How were they arrived at in their day? The process was different in different periods. At first they were based on the theological outlook of the early Middle Ages and, on the musical-technical side, deduced abstractly from the numerical theories of consonance which had been inherited from classical Greek philosophy. As learned musical practice became more widespread, these musical-technical theories, correct as far as they went, needed to be expanded. During the early 13th Century they had to provide the basis for new musical styles which were becoming established through the creative efforts of individuals or schools of composers, efforts inspired by a changing and increasing social demand; such were, for example, the styles of the Notre Dame organa. The Florentina Ars Nova produced also its theorists in the early 14th Century. The influence of folk-music on composed music had its repercussions with the development of gymel and subsequently of English discant and the continental faux-bourdon, for the practical and systematic mastery of which were designed such treatises as those of Leonel Power on Discant, "for hem (them) that will be singers or makers or techers", and the Scottish Anonymous on "Faburdun" (S. M. Add. 4911). In these treatises no theological basis for musical practice is propounded; the authors concern themselves solely with musical-technical problems. Both are explicit in their statements of general musical principles and precise in their explanations of the practical application of these principles. The Scottish Anonymous begins as follows:

> Quhat is Faburdun? Faburdun is ane melodius kynd of harmony quhilk dois transmut and brek sympill noits in figurs colorat be numars trinar and binar conform to ye way of music mensurall. Quhow many kyndis of faburdun are nemmit? Four. Quhow sall the first kynd of faburdun be knawin? Be rewills and exemplis.

Then follow a number of rules for the transposition of the plain-song melody from the "propir seit" into the highest voice part, for the modifications required by musica ficta, etc. Rules five and six are expressed as follows:

> The fyfst rewill is: Suppois the plane sang be uprasit fro ye propir seit, or modulat in ye propir seit. The thrid part of faburdun, callit ye counter, sall ay be sett in ferds (fourths) beneth ye plane sang and ye thrid abown the baritonant. Except quhan the baritonant makkis ye closing puncts down in the octawe beneth ye plane sang, than the closing puncts of the said counter sall clois in the fyfst abow ye baritonant. Of the quhilk counter ye modulaturs sall sing nan uther noits bot ye same noits of the plane sang all in ferds beneth ye same.

> The saxt rewill is: If the finall noit of any vers, hyme, antiphon or respond be nocht flexible to resawe a unplesand clois it is admittit be all musicians to augment the finall with ane sympill noit eftir

the last noit of ye plane sang for ye making of ye last closing punct plesand.

> The first exemplill is: That ye plane sang is all extendit and modulat in diapason abown the propir seit and ye baritonant is sett and modulat all in saxta beneth ye extendit plane sang. Except that all ye closing puncts pf same dois to ye octawe descend. To the quhilk eftir ye finall noitt of the plane sang for decoring of the closing punct ane sympill noit is augmentit.

As a result of the increasing importance of secular music and the beginnings in the Renaissance of a scientific world-outlook the authors of treatises on composition no longer sought a theological basis for their general principles. Zarlino in his *Instituzione harmoniche*, first published in 1558, attempts to base his principles on scientific laws. Zarlino regarded music as a reflection of nature and concerned himself with the means of the musical reflection of human emotions. In his 32nd Chapter on "How the harmonies are adapted to the words placed beneath them" he wrote as follows:

> For if in speech, whether by way of narrative or of imitation (and these occur in speech), matters may be treated that are joyful or mournful, and grave or without gravity, and again modest or lascivious, we must also make a choice of a harmony and a rhythm similar to the nature of the matters contained in the speech in order that from the combination of these things, put together with proportion, may result a melody suited to the purpose.*

There then follows a lengthy paragraph giving the kind of intervals, melodic movement and rhythmic character suited to the expression of various emotions.

What Zarlino did on the practical side for the Italian School was done for English music by Thomas Morley in his *Plain and Easy Introduction to Practical Music*, first published in 1597. In his foreword "To the courteous reader" the author explains his aim as "in some sort to further the studies of them who (being indued with good natural wits, and well inclined to learn that divine Art of Music) are destitute of sufficient masters." The book begins with an explanation of musical notation; this introductory section leads to the main part, an admirable text-book of composition, comprising both general principles and practical examples. The principles and practice are those of

*Strunk: *Source Readings in Music History*. (Faber)

Morley's immediate predecessors. His intentions and difficulties are well expressed in another passage of the foreword.

> "Taking therefore those precepts which being a child I learned, and laying them together in order, I began to compare them with some other of the same kind, set down by some late writers: But then I was in a worse case than before. For I found such diversity betwixt them, that I knew not which part said truest, or whom I might best believe. Then was I forced to run to the works of many, both strangers and Englishmen (whose labours together with their names had been buried with me in perpetual oblivion, if it had not been for this occasion) for a solution and clearing of my doubt. But to my great grief, then did I see the most part of mine own precepts false and easy to be confuted by the works of Taverner, Fairfax, Cooper, and infinite more, whose names it would be too tedious to set down in this place."

Morley's solution is to explain the practice generally followed by his greatest predecessors and contemporaries. He does not attempt any kind of theoretical basis for the rules advocated. Where he criticises or allows deviations he makes it clear that these are his own opinions, arrived at for this or that reason.

Subsequent writers of text-books on composition fall into two categories. There are on the one side the theoreticians, who, like Zarlino, attempt to found musical laws on more general principles, usually mathematical. Rameau, with his *Treatise on Harmony reduced to its natural princples* (1722) and Hindemith with his *Craft of Musical Composition* (1937) are examples of this.

Neither Rameau nor Hindemith see the scientific laws underlying music as ends in themselves. Like Zarlino, they see as the function of music, the expression of human emotions. Rameau in his Treatise writes as follows:

> "It is certain that harmony can arouse in us different passions, depending on the particular harmonies that are employed. There are harmonies that are sad, languishing, tender, agreeable, gay, and striking . . . . . . For the rest, a good musician ought to surrender himself to all the characters he wishes to depict and, like a skilful actor, put himself in the place of the speaker, imagine himself in the localities where the different events he wishes to represent occur, and take in these the same interest as those most

concerned; he ought to be a good speaker, at least by nature; and he ought to know when the voice should be raised or lowered, by more or by less, in order to adapt to this his melody, his harmony, his modulation, and his movement."*

Hindemith, arguing for the most complete understanding of musical laws, writes thus: "Is not an immense mastery of the medium needed to translate into tones what the heart dictates?"

On the other hand there are the more empirical teachers, who, like Morley, content themselves with advocating rules of procedure, which, they believe, summarise the practice of their immediate predecessors. Such was Johann Joseph Fux, whose *Gradus ad Parnassum*, first published in 1725, formed the basis of the teaching of so-called "strict counterpoint" until the end of the first world war. In the "Author's Foreword to the Reader" he writes as follows.

> "Some people will perhaps wonder why I have undertaken to write about music, there being so many works by outstanding men who have treated the subject most thoroughly and learnedly; and more especially why I should be doing so just at this time when music has become almost arbitrary and composers refuse to be bound by any rules and principles, detesting the very name of school and law like death itself. To such I want to make my purpose clear . . . . . .
> Medicine is given to the sick, and not to those who are in good health. However, my efforts do not tend — nor do I credit myself with the strength — to stem the course of a torrent rushing precipitously beyond its bounds. I do not believe that I can call back composers from the unrestrained insanity of their writing to normal standards. Let each follow his own counsel. My object is to help young persons who want to learn. I knew and still know many who have fine talents and are most anxious to study; however, lacking means and a teacher, they cannot realise their ambition, but remain, as it were, forever desperately athirst."**

Fux's intention was to provide such "young people who are most anxious to study" with a methodical practical introduction into the

*Strunk: *Source Readings in Music History*. pp. 272-274. (Faber).
**Fux: *Steps to Parnassus*. Trans. Mann (Dent.)

most completely worked out system of composition which had existed up to his own lifetime. His designation of some of his contemporary composers as "unrestrainedly insane in their writings" proves that he did not regard the musical conditions of his own day as unified by a consistently worked-out system. Thus his own day could not provide the young composer with a firm foundation from which to develop. Fux based his *Gradus ad Parnassum* on the style of Palestrina. The fact that he did not present the style quite correctly, that he disallowed some of the practices of the style and on the other hand introduced idioms of his own day which were foreign to it, does not detract from the debt which our musical culture owes to him. His method provided the correct solution of the problem in his day, and his application of it was entirely admirable in all but a few unessential details. Mozart, Haydn, Beethoven, Rossini, Cherubini, Berlioz, Meyerbeer, Chopin, Paganini, Mendlessohn, Liszt and Brahms all learned counterpoint by working through the *Gradus ad Parnassum.*

Among all these illustrious names that of J. S. Bach is conspicuously absent. Bach was already himself an experienced teacher when the "Gradus" first appeared. It is known that, although he esteemed Fux as a composer, he did not agree with his method as a teacher. Bach's own method, which omitted all contact with the style of the 16th Century, is, in my opinion, the correct way of teaching the harmony and counterpoint which forms the common basis of 18th and 19th century music. But the mastery of this type of harmony and counterpoint should not be considered the only technical study necessary to the composer of to-day, as Bach believed it to be as far as his own pupils were concerned. This question will be referred to later on.

During the second half of the 18th and early 19th Centuries the study of composition comprised the harmony of Rameau and the counterpoint of Fux as developed in the works of the student's immediate predecessors. There does not seem to have been any systematic study of musical form apart from fugue. Music of an earlier period was considered archaic. Beethoven knew of earlier styles only the 48 Preludes and Fugues of Bach and some concerti grossi and oratorios of Handel. This situation was universal until, in the middle of the 19th Century, Mendlessohn rediscoverred the Saint Matthew Passion. The effect of this rediscovery was to arouse interest in so-called "free counterpoint", that of the late 17th and early 18th Centuries. "Strict counterpoint" became a special discipline. Text-books in both types of counterpoint as well as in harmony appeared in every country. Those in strict counterpoint multiplied the anachronisms of Fux at the whim of the particular author, those in free counterpoint claimed to expound Bach's practice but hedged it about with abstract disallowances, either the result of the author's personal predilections or made on grounds of pedagogic expediency, which in such cases was permitted to become the criterion of what to allow and what to forbid. There were exceptions, of course. Balakirev in his work with the Russian Five introduced the revolutionary method of the formal and harmonic analysis of contemporary works, especially those of Liszt, Berlioz and Schumann. In the last decades of the 19th Century the study of sonata form began.

This general method, if such it deserves to be called, sufficed in countries where there existed a flourishing and continuous national musical tradition, countries such as Germany, Austria, Italy and France. The freshly developing nationalisms of Poland, Bohemia and Russia had such vitality, their music was so closely linked to the social life of the people, that their composers were able to strike out new paths, developed from their own folk-music and from the common European tradition, but not stifled by the latter.

But in Britain the pervading influence was that of an abstract Teutonism. Our musical life, dominated after the death of Purcell by continental practitioners, became in the late 19th Century the prey of continental theory also, the influence of Germany being paramount. Frederick Corder at the Royal Academy of Music plunged his students into the ocean of Wagner. Sir Charles Stanford at the Royal College of Music taught the technique of Brahms, in whose works he believed music had reached its highest degree of organisation, though at the same time he introduced the study of 16th Century counterpoint, the value of which as a discipline was only then beginning to be appreciated. Furthermore Stanford tried to interest his students in Irish, Scottish and English folk-music, the treasures of which were being made generally available for the first time, in some cases rescued from oblivion in this very period.

These were the conditions in which I, innocent of any theory but enamoured of musical art, began in 1918 my studies in composition with four years under Corder at the Royal Academy of Music. After this I became a pupil of Dr John Ireland. When, in 1925, I started to teach composition myself, I was still enjoying the privelege of Dr Ireland's stimulating instructions, which he showered generously upon many of our younger British composers. Looking back, I cannot but congratulate myself on my good fortune. Corder and Stanford were undoubtedly the greatest teachers of their generation in Britain, and through Dr Ireland I received Stanford's tradition, handed on through the personality of one of our foremost creative musicians.

As a beginner in teaching my aim was to transmit such knowledge as I had acquired along the general lines practised by Dr Ireland. But soon the chaos of musical life which had been precipitated in 1895 by Debussy's masterpiece *L'Aprèsmidi d'une Faune* began to make itself felt even in Britain, which was in 1920 a relatively backward country in both the theory and practice of music. By 1930 we were aware of the fact that the more or less orderly and unified development of music through the 17th, 18th and 19th Centuries was over. In its place was a chaotic conglomeration of musical styles, many of which had nothing in common with one another, all being in sharp contradiction to one or other of the basic principles of 19th Century music. The teaching of composition in general took a turn away from the study of the traditional disciplines of harmony and counterpoint. Students were subjected either to the idiosyncracy of the particular teacher or to the dogmatism of one or other of the new systems of composition, which were propounded by rival theoreticians as methods of overcoming the musical crisis, but none of which has as yet achieved anything like general or even increasing acceptance. In these conditions some teachers contented themselves merely with trying not to interfere with the students' individualities; the latter were often taught no traditional disciplines, as they would not find them useful in the expression of their modern souls.

In these circumstances it seemed to me essential to devise a method of teaching composition which would equip the student with a mastery of technique, shield him from the idiosyncracy of his teacher, and protect him from the otherwise overpowering influence of German music (and in the process from other only slightly less potent influences such as French impressionism and post-impressionism, Béla Bartók, and the cosmopolitan styles and theories of Stravinsky, Hindemith and Schoenberg, all alike alien to the historical tradition of British music). I believe that I have now devised such a method, and I believe it to be the correct method of teaching and learning composition.

The object of my method is in general the same as that which inspired Fux in his *Gradus*, that is to say, to provide the "young person who wants to learn" with a clear knowledge and practical mastery of the techniques of those past periods of musical history which achieved general acceptance in their day; in particulat I pay attention to the development of our English music. But in carrying out the method I start earlier and finish later than Fux did. Thus instead of beginning with the 16th Century I start with Gregorian Plainchant and proceed through the so-called strict or parallel organum to free organum, then through English discant to the developed polyphony of the 15th and 16th Centuries. I introduce English folk-music from the beginning of the course of study. A difficulty arises with the close of the 16th Century. The period of transition between the disintegration of the modes and the final triumph of the major and minor scales contains many confusing features. It is unfortunate for this method — as far as English students are concerned — that Purcell falls into this period. It is possible, however, to use his chaconnes as examples of variation form. The harmony of the major and minor period must, however, it seems to me, be studied in the chorales of J. S. Bach. The next stage is therefore a systematic study of these, during which the whole harmonic vocabulary is learnt through Bach's own figured basses, and others worked out from his chorales.

By this time the student, with his knowledge of 16th Century technique, will be able to take in his stride the added complications of Bach's style in its entirety. He will have been spared the deadening impact on his musical taste and enthusiasm of writing exercises in which, in the first chapter, one triad in root position follows another (a way of composing known only among the most primitive chorale composers such as Osiander, and never likely to return), then, in the next chapter but one on the cadential and passing six-four chords, exercises in which the author of the text-book has thoughtfully arranged for the former harmony (fortunately a rarity in the classics) to appear with an unnatural frequency, and then, most absurd of all, by exercises on passing notes, where otherwise innocuous harmonic progressions are to be rendered fatuous by the addition of a continuous flow of insipid unessential notes. The overwhelming advantage of the historical method of study now becomes apparent. Throughout his study the composer is occupied solely with the creation of complete musical works instead of with a sort of potted music, which no composer of any period has ever dreamed of writing.

Bach's Inventions then provide the basis for the student's study of the 18th Century contrapuntal practice, leading to the study of fugue. The formal principles of the Vienna Classics up to and including Beethoven must then be mastered.

At this point I have hitherto called a halt. Armed with this technique and understanding of style, the student is equipped to search for himself among the harmonic developments of the late 19th Century and the theoretical and practical chaos of the 20th. His early occupation with the styles up to the 16th Century and with folk-music will inoculate him against the otherwise overpowering impact of the German and Austrian music of the last two hundred and fifty years, which assails him daily as he practises his instrument and listens to concerts and operas.

It will be clear, I hope, that this method of studying composition is equally applicable — but with important modifications of practical detail — to students of any nationality. A French composer would substitute for English Descant and English folk-song the organa of the Notre Dame School, Machaut and the Early Netherland composers, and French folk-song; a Czech would pay special attention to the Hussite songs, the early Bohemian polyphonists and the Bohemian and Moravian folk-songs.

In conclusion I have one point to clarify. In referring to the chaos of the 20th Century, I do not wish it to be inferred that I regard all the conflicting styles and methods of composing to-day as equally misguided. But the following statement can hardly be disputed. The two most influential and at the same time mutually contradictory musical theories of to-day, Schoenberg's 12-Tone System, now known as Serial Dodecaphony, and Hindemith's theoretical re-establishment of tonality as a basic and therefore unavoidable ingredient in the fabric of musical art, are neither as yet generally accepted methods of composing, as were the methods analysed and given theoretical foundation by Zarlino and Rameau in their respective periods. Schoenberg and Hindemith cannot both be right. They may both be wrong or partially wrong. Indeed, I believe the last to be the case. And out of this belief I have developed the particular technique which I have practised myself fitfully for the last twenty-seven and systematically for the last twelve years. But as it has been my aim to devise a systematic method of learning composition which will render the student independent of the musical predilections or even of the world-outlook of the teacher, I exclude in principle from the general course this technique of thematic composing as I practise it personally. For the same reason I refrain in this article from entering into the field of to-day's basic musical controversies (of which Schoenberg versus Hindemith is not the most fundamental), not because I regard such problems as either unimportant or insoluble, but because they are in principle outside the terms of reference which my treatment of the present subject prescribes.

5

The greatness of Beethoven

The greatness of Beethoven has never been in question. In 1792, when Beethoven was 21 years old, he left his birthplace, Bonn, on a second visit to Vienna. His friends inscribed their farewells in an album. Count Waldstein, a young aristocrat and amateur of music, to whom Beethoven subsequently dedicated one of his most famous piano sonatas, wrote as follows:

Dear Beethoven, you are travelling to Vienna in fulfilment of your long cherished wish. The genius of Mozart is still weeping and bewailing the death of her favourite. With the inexhaustible Haydn she found a refuge, but no occupation, and is now waiting to leave him and join herself to someone else. Labour assiduously and receive Mozart's spirit from the hands of Haydn.

Your true friend, Waldstein.
Bonn, October 29th, 1792.

Beethoven's funeral in Vienna on March 29th, 1827, was attended by a vast number of people; the coffin was borne by eight leading musicians of the city and surrounded by thirty-six torch-bearers, including the composer, Schubert, and the famous piano virtuoso and teacher, Carl Czerny, familiar to though perhaps not exactly beloved by millions of children on account of his innumerable piano studies. The crowd surrounding the funeral procession was so enormous that soldiers were called in to clear a way through the streets; even so it took an hour and a half to cover the short distance between Beethoven's house and the church.

As a professional musician Beethoven enjoyed uninterrupted recognition from a very early age. At eleven years old he was appointed deputy organist in the court chapel of the Elector of Bonn by his teacher, Neefe; from then on until the last days of his life he was continuously and successfully occupied with musical composition, with performing as a piano virtuoso, with teaching the piano, and with the supervision of the publication and performance of his works. Throughout his life he enjoyed the personal friendship, appreciation and financial support of a large number of musical amateurs from the aristocracy and rising middle class, and in his later years, when he openly espoused with his musical works the cause of the German and Austrian peoples against the Emperor Napoleon, the whole populace of Vienna came to regard him as their own friend and representative. In 1813 a concert took place, the programme of which included the first performances of the 7th Symphony in A major and the tone poem entitled "Wellington's Victory". There is a story that Beethoven was strolling the next morning through the streets of Vienna, when he met some girls selling cherries, who offered him some from their baskets; he was about to pay, but they refused to accept the money, after hearing, as they said, his beautiful music the night before.

Within a few years of Beethoven's death his life, personality and music became the subject of innumerable studies, biographical, psychological, aesthetic and even philosophic. He was then and is still generally recognised as the greatest musical composer of all time. It is nowhere disputed that the appeal of his music has always reached the widest circles of music lovers in every country where European symphonic, operatic and chamber music has been made available. Millions of people listen to his compositions every year and the number is still constantly increasing one hundred and twenty-five years after his death. Despite the fact that most of his music is very difficult to perform adequately, hundreds of thousands of amateur instrumentalists struggle year after year with his piano, violin and cello works, and the string quartets and trios. He did not compose many choral works apart from his greatest masterpieces, the Ninth Symphony and the Missa Solennis in D; and none of his choral works is complete without the accompaniment of a symphony orchestra. For this reason our choral singers in small choirs (and these comprise by far the most numerous class of practising amateur musicians) have no chance to get to know his music as performers, since, except for the "Prisoners' Chorus" from the opera *Fidelio,* there is nothing for them to tackle. How then are we to explain the immense and growing popularity of this composer, whose works are so comparatively difficult of access? What does he say to men and women all over the world which they want to listen to, which seems to mean something to them that matters, something which helps them to solve the problems facing them in their day-to-day struggles?

The explanation is by no means mysterious or difficult to understand. All that is needed is an approach to Beethoven's life and works without preconceived ideas as to what his music does or ought to do. Beethoven has himself given us the key in the records of his conversations, in his actions, in his choice of subjects for many of his works, and in his method of treatment of the texts he chose and of his musical material.

It is true that this key opens a door into a region, unexpected by many musical enthusiasts and unwelcome to not a few. Beethoven does not fit into the theory which teaches that music is one thing and life another, that the value of a musical work depends exclusively upon the quality of the musical ideas in themselves, the way in which they relate to one another, and the originality or aptness of the treatment, irrespective of the effect which the composer desired to produce on his audience; and conversely, that its value depends not at all upon the experiences and outlook of the composer in his life in human society or his desire to communicate his feelings and thoughts to his fellow men and women.

With Beethoven what he had to say dictated how he said it. His pointers in this direction are so unmistakable that protagonists of an art for art's sake musical theory have been driven, either to omit them from all mention, deride them as insignificant, or deplore them as unfortunate lapses from aesthetic rectitude, which Beethoven would no doubt have avoided, had he enjoyed the benefit of the particular theoretician's advice.

Beethoven's first biographer, Anton Schindler, saw the composer nearly every day from early in 1815 until his death in 1827. He attached himself to Beethoven with a loyalty and persistence which were remarkable, performing for him innumerable small commissions and acting as a kind of devoted unpaid secretary. . He was certainly the person who knew Beethoven better than anyone else. At one point in his biography he wrote as follows:

We must now turn to a curious preoccupation of Beethoven's, curious because it concerned not so much the musical field as that of general political life. We must accustom ourselves to follow our tone-poet into this region, so foreign to his own field of operations, because one side of his nature drove him irresistibly in this direction, and set a political stamp on many of his outward actions.

In another paragraph Schindler lists six different reasons why Beethoven was "a consistent opponent of Austrian state policy, of the government, and of the Imperial court."

In an article which has recently appeared in the magazine *Music and Society*, published in the German Democratic Republic, Dr Georg Knepler points out that Schindler, while correctly stating the fact that Beethoven was deeply interested in political affairs, misunderstood its full significance. Knepler writes: "Schindler's opinion that this region was 'so foreign to Beethoven's field of operations' must now give way before the realisation that Beethoven's musical creation in many of its technical, melodic, harmonic and formal aspects was moulded by the message of his work, further, that this message was the result of Beethoven's understanding of political events."

Of Beethoven's life-long interest in politics there is no doubt. In 1789, in his 19th year, he was still living in Bonn, a few miles from the French border. The storming of the Bastille on July 14th of that year roused tremendous enthusiasm in the Rheinland territory. Beethoven is known to have heard the lectures of Eulogius Schneider, Professor of Philosophy in the newly founded Bonn University, who greeted the ideals and heroism of the French Revolution with fiery enthusiasm. More than this, Beethoven's name appears among the subscribers to a collection of the Professor's revolutionary poems.

The idea that the French Revolution would usher in a new period of freedom for mankind was Beethoven's guiding belief until the year 1804. During the winter of 1803-04 Beethoven was mainly occupied in composing the 3rd Symphony in E flat. On the original title page the work was designated as "Grand Symphony Napoleon Bonaparte by Mr Louis van Beethoven". In May, 1804, Napoleon assumed the title of Emperor of France. When the news of this event reached Beethoven he immediately tore off the original title page and renamed the Symphony "Eroica" or "the Heroic", dedicating it to Prince Lobkowitz, one of his most enthusiastic patrons among the Austrian aristocrats. The crowning of Napoleon as Emperor was not for Beethoven merely a sign of personal aggrandisement by an individual. He understood from it that a development had taken place, which had fundamentally altered the direction in which the French Revolution was originally leading, away from the liberty, equality and fraternity of the first period, to a new form of despotism, this time that of the French big business class. From this moment onwards Beethoven realised with astonishing political insight that Napoleon and Napoleon's France had become the enemy. From now on he fought for the liberation of the peoples of Europe from the control of France with the same energy with which he had formerly supported the French Revolution.

His next major works were the opera *Fidelio,* the first version of which was completed in 1805, and the 5th Symphony in C minor, begun in 1805 and finished in 1807.

In *Fidelio* Beethoven chose a subject of the very greatest significance in the fight for freedom. The story is as follows. Florestan, "the man of noble character who fights for truth" as Beethoven described him, is illegally detained in prison by Pizarro, the representative of reaction and corruption, who, in the fight against truth does not intend to stop even at murder. Florestan is rescued by the heroism and resourcefulness of his wife, Leonora, who, disguised as a boy, works as the assistant to the chief gaoler of the prison, and finally gains access to the deep dungeon in which Florestan is incarcerated on the pretext of helping the gaoler to dig the grave of the prisoner, who is in danger of death from exhaustion or from the hand of Pizarro himself. Armed with a pistol which she intends to use against Pizarro, Leonora reaches her husband's side and rallies him. Just as Pizarro enters the dungeon in order to murder Florestan the sound of trumpets announcing the arrival of the Governor of the province stays Pizarro's hand, as he realises that he will be unable in a few minutes to hide the murder from his superior. Florestan is freed and with a mighty expression of joy in the triumph of heroism in the cause of truth and justice the opera finishes. During the opera occurs the "Prisoners' Chorus". This is the longest single musical number in the opera. From a dramatic point of view it does not advance the action at all. Leonora, or "Fidelio" as she is known to the gaoler, persuades him to allow the prisoners out of their cells into the open air of the prison courtyard. With much trepidation he does so. The prisoners issue from their cells, scarcely able to believe that they are breathing the air of heaven again. Nervously they emerge and fearfully retreat, with scarcely time to raise their voices in a chorus of joy at seeing once again the blue sky and greenery of nature. In this chorus, one of the most beautiful pieces of music ever written, Beethoven has expressed the piteous plight of the unjustly imprisoned.

But in the opera as a whole he is not content only to express sorrow for injustice, but shows how an unyielding and intelligently conducted fight against tyranny can bring it down.

His next major work, the 5th Symphony in C minor, was begun in 1805 and finished two years later. Here Beethoven made an attempt to express the struggle of man for truth and liberty. The summons from the outside world, "fate knocking at the door", rouses man to action, then through the contemplation of the second movement and the uneasy misgivings of the scherzo, he triumphs in the radiant optimism of the Finale.

It may be that some people will feel some doubts as to the possibility of penetrating accurately to the feelings Beethoven intended to portray in his purely instrumental works. And indeed it is no easy matter in many cases. But that Beethoven intended his works, instrumental as well as vocal, to convey his feelings to the hearer there is no doubt. Schindler has reported in his biography that Beethoven was planning a new edition of his piano works, in which he intended to "disclose the poetical ideas living within the various works, by which the tone-poet had allowed himself to be guided." "Beethoven", said Schindler, "had aimed at setting forth these poetical ideas in such a way that their artistic truth appeared without words of explanation being necessary. On one occasion, however, Beethoven consented to explain the slow movement of the piano sonata in D major, Op 10, as depicting the condition of soul of a man beset by melancholy, with all the varied nuances of light and shade which might colour a picture of this state of soul." In some other works "anyone", Beethoven maintained, "could recognise the struggle between two principles in the form of a dialogue." In further confirmation of this intention of Beethoven's, Ferdinand Ries, Beethoven's favourite piano pupil and one of his most intimate friends, stated that to his knowledge Beethoven often thought of a particular object, i.e. some concrete matter, experience or happening, when composing.

These explanations by Beethoven are extremely important as guides to our true understanding of his instrumental music. They make it clear, without a shadow of doubt, that Beethoven intended his music to be understood as an expression of human feelings and thoughts, and even as a way of overcoming the inclination to a hopeless resignation, which the shattered hopes and tragic outcome of the French Revolution might otherwise engender. There are a large number of works in which the struggle and violent contradictions of the first movement are triumphantly resolved in the last movement, as in the 5th Symphony in C minor already referred to.

But to return to the development of Beethoven's political views. His enthusiastic support of the Allies, including Austria, against Napoleon continued until the Congress of Vienna in 1815. He had been disgusted by the shameful peace signed with Napoleon by the German princes, under which they undertook to supply him with their conscripted serfs and other military forces for his attack on Russia. But the Congress of Vienna placed the forces of reaction once again in control of France, Germany and Austria. All chance of achieving liberty, equality and fraternity seemed farther away than ever. In 1815 Beethoven wrote: "I am broken down in health, a state of affairs to which our political situation has contributed not a little; we can expect no improvement, in fact things get worse every day. Everything around us condemns us to silence." This last remark was a reference to the fact that Vienna had become the headquarters of the spying and police network of Metternich, the Austrian Chancellor.

This new situation must have been an even more shattering disappointment to Beethoven than the betrayal of the expressed aims of the French Revolution had been. It is most instructive at this point to compare his reactions with those of Schubert, now 18 years old, but already the composer of such masterpieces as the "Erl-King". In a poem which Schubert himself wrote at the time, he has left us a description of the task he would set himself in his musical works. He speaks of the "youth of the peoples", now unhappily past, and bewails his own time as one of "dusty deedlessness". Thus he can set himself in his music only the following task:

> To paint those times of power and deeds now gone,
> So as to lessen by a little the bitter pain
> That never can forget that past's betrayal,
> And thus accept our present fate.

This despair breaks out in many of Schubert's works. With Beethoven the situation is quite opposite. Not despair but an even more embittered hostility to the Austrian Government and Court, not the abandonment of his struggle through his music for a better world, but a new method of struggle. This reached expression in Beethoven's two most massive works, the Ninth Symphony and the Missa Solennis in D. Both were written in response to requests from outside. The Royal Philharmonic Society of London had previously tried to commission symphonies from Beethoven, but without success. On this occasion their invitation to provide a symphony was accepted, and Beethoven was occupied with it from 1817-23, the *Choral Symphony* in D minor being the result. In this work Beethoven abandoned the attempt to convey his message by instrumental means only, he determined to avoid all possibility of being misunderstood. To this end he chose the "Ode to Joy" by Schiller, a call for the universal brotherhood of all mankind. In this gigantic work the struggles of the first movement are finally resolved in the choral finale which urges men and women to embrace one another in universal brotherhood and thus usher in a new era in human history. Here Beethoven speaks to the people directly; he has lost faith in the power or intention of heroic individuals or ruling-class governments to benefit mankind.

In the summer of 1818 Beethoven's former pupil and faithful patron, the Archduke Rudolph, was appointed Archbishop of Olmuetz. Beethoven was invited to contribute a grand mass for the installation. He set to work at once, but as things turned out he took five years to complete the work, so that it proved to be too late for the installation by about three years. It might seem that a setting of the words of the Mass could hardly produce a work which would carry Beethoven's message forward. But the opposite proved to be the case. On the one hand, awe at the glory and wonder of man together with the expression of a burning hope for his life in the future, on the other hand a heart-rending cry for the establishment of peace on earth are the two most intensely conveyed aspects of his message in this greatest musical masterpiece of all time. Without a detailed exposition of the musical structure of the work, it is not possible to make this statement entirely convincing. Briefly, Beethoven achieves by the extraordinary care and expressiveness with which, in the Creed, he leads up to and underlines the words *"et homo, homo factus est"* "and was made man, man" and the ecstatic climax at the words *"et vitam venturi"* "and the life of the future". At the beginning of the Agnus Dei, the final movement of the Mass, Beethoven himself wrote on the score "Prayer for inner and outer Peace". He precedes the words *dona nobis pacem* ("give us peace") with an orchestral interlude depicting the sounds of far off military music, drums and trumpet calls which come gradually nearer, until one of the soloists breaks forth into an agonised cry of *"Agnus Dei, qui tollis peccata mundi, dona nobis pacem* ("Oh Lamb of God, that taketh away the sins of the world, grant us peace"). There could be no musical treatment which more unmistakably conveys Beethoven's intention that it was against the evils of war as well as the pains of the soul's unrest that his cry was directed.

Despite the evidence in support of the theory that Beethoven desired to convey through his music human feelings, and that he succeeded in this desire, there are yet opponents of it. They usually argue that in Beethoven's very latest works, which were exclusively instrumental, there is no trace of an extra-musical content, that his earlier works were something in the nature of youthful indiscretions, and that it is by his latest fruits alone that he should be judged and understood. A moment's thought will dispel the absurdutiy of this argument. Beethoven was only 57 years old when he died in 1827, four years only after the completion of the Mass; moreover it is well known that he was full of plans for new compositions, including a second opera. There is thus absolutely no ground for the supposition that he had turned his back upon vocal music, or changed in any way his intentions to convey to mankind his own optimism for the future and his courage in carrying on such an indomitable struggle.

Of course he did not always occupy himself exclusively with the most profound social problems. In his piano and other instrumental works he was concerned with the expression of more personal emotions, and their struggle with one another. Knepler has pointed out in the above-mentioned article, how Beethoven treats the expression of melancholy, despair, and resignation, emotions which were particularly widely experienced in the epoch in which his later years were passed. He is concerned to express in his music not only these emotions but the overcoming of them, either through a joyful, liberating finale, or by means of the expression of "inner peace", not the passive self-deceit of resignation, but a lofty calmness, full of inner energy, a state of mind from which a fresh outward thrust can be initiated. The last movement of his latest piano sonata, Opus 111 in C minor, is an example of this solution of the problem.

At this point the theoreticians of emptiness in music, those who declare that music is in its very nature incapable of expressing anything at all, whether a human emotion or thought, or a phenomenon of nature (and since Hanslick in 1864 there has developed a school of musical theorists with this outlook, headed recently by the composer, Igor Stravinsky) — at this point such people bring up what they believe to be their final and unanswerable objection. How, they ask, can combinations of air waves of varying frequency and strength possibly incorporate or convey a feeling or a thought, which are interior phenomena of the human consciousness? It is true, they may perhaps continue, that spoken words are also air waves, but the sounds have been associated by usage with certain phenomena of the outside world or the interior world of consciousness. Thus if I say "that chair is brown" or "I feel depressed" the particular airwaves produced can be interpreted by those other people who have learnt to associate these sounds with particular things. "Chair", "brownness", "depression", "I", are all recognisable and known sounds to those men and women who are familiar with the particular language. But this, our opponents will argue, is not true of music. The "words" of music, the combinations of sound which make up the musical sentences, are so ambiguous as to be uninterpretable, untranslatable. Even if the composer intends them to convey a certain feeling, his intentions are fruitless and foredoomed to failure; each hearer will translate the words of this language as he or she feels inclined. Thus the true appreciation of music, our opponents say, consists *not* in understanding its content, for it has none, but in following and enjoying the way in which the composer has treated the musical themes and subject-matter, the variety of harmony, rhythm and tone-colour, the balance of the formal construction, and the development of the themes themselves during the course of the work. Beethoven, they say, is great because his ingenuity in all these directions in indeed great. The arresting quality of his themes, the strength of his harmony, his powerful rhythm and beautiful tone-variety, his command of monumental formal construction and ability to develop his thematic material convincingly, all these characteristics entitle him to our deepest admiration as a truly great composer. The circumstance, our opponents would add, that he happened to imagine that he was in fact conveying his feelings and ideas of great importance to mankind is in the nature of a harmless foible on his part, which did not appear seriously to impair his musical faculties, and may in fact have been the driving force which enabled him to reach the high state of mental concentration required for artistic creations so vast, brilliant and sustained.

To some people it may seem idle to reply to such an apparently absurd point of view. Yet there may be some who will ask themselves whether there may not be something in it. Certainly music consists solely of vibrations of air waves of different strength and frequencies. If it is a language at all, it is certainly less precisely interpretable, translatable, than the languages of speech. Doubts may creep in. And then we may find ourselves asking whether it is worth our while to bother about such dubious and seemingly obscure forms of communication as the musical compositions of a German composer, more than one hundred and fifty years dead. Even if we enjoy listening to many of them, may that not be because they "take us out of ourselves" and make us forget for the time being our pressing problems? May they not be an avenue of escapism?

There is no doubt that to the vast majority of listeners and also performers, both professional and amateur, in Britain to-day, instrumental music is precisely that and little more. The hysterical screams of enthusiasm of the Promenade public at the Royal Albert Hall, London, are evidence that a large section of the musical public treats music as a means of luxurious relaxation for their pent-up emotions, a kind of bath salts of the soul. The somewhat nebulous character of the language of music makes this possible, even where the composer's intentions are opposite. Beethoven's music is certainly not of a type which lends itself easily to such usage; for this the later romantics, such as Wagner, Richard Strauss, Mahler, Cèsar Franck, and even Tchaikovsky are more suited. But some people can wallow even in Beethoven.

It is thus essential that the art for art's sake theory of music should be shown up for the superficial and unscientific nonsense which it is.

The whole theory crumbles when music is viewed in its totality as a part of human social activity; and there is no other way in which it can be viewed except through the mud-coloured spectacles of unconscious prejudice. If music consisted solely of the European instrumental music of the 18th and 19th Centuries, the art for art's sake theory would be more plausible than it is (though it would be incorrect, even in this case). But this is only one type of music. Music has existed since the most primitive tribal social conditions. Curt Sachs, the greatest living authority on the music of primitive peoples and ancient civilisations, sums up his lifetime of research into this field with the words: "Music began with singing." He stated moreover that the most elementary music consists of melodies of two tones only. This primitive music is an important part of the life of all tribal societies, it is much more actively practised by all members of the tribe than is the case in any civilised society nowadays. How strange that in a society so near the borderline of extinction in the struggle against nature so much time and energy should be devoted to an occupation so apparently useless as music! Music must have a great use-value for such societies. Think for a moment of the way of working of primitive communities. A great deal of the heavy work of the tribe, the making of protective palisades with trunks of trees, boulders, etc., is done necessarily by groups of people using their hands and arms. The tasks of raising and lugging heavy logs must be performed communally. It so happens that our vocal chords produce involuntarily sounds of higher or lower pitch, according to the amount of exertion we are putting out at the moment of expiration. The communally performed tasks of lugging would be accompanied by grunts and shouts; it would be discovered, perhaps by accident, that the necessary movements could be co-ordinated better by synchronised grunts and shouts. A preparatory shout would precede the co-ordinated movement of all taking part. This maximum moment of effort would also be accompanied by another vocal sound, which, as it was emitted at a moment of such intense exertion, would tend to be of higher pitch than the preparatory shout, to which, however, it would be connected rhythmically. Thus would have originated many, perhaps all of the melodies of two tones. These melodies are thus seen to be the vocal expression by the human organism of conditions of lesser and greater muscular, nervous and emotional tension within that organism.

From melodies of two tones have developed more complicated tunes of five, eight, even of many tones. The combination of melodies with notes of lower and higher pitch, later the imitation of voices by instruments and consequent development up to the vast forms of our present-day concert and operatic music, this unfolding of the possibilities of music as human society developed is only a vastly increased variety of sounds, expressing lesser or greater degrees of muscular, nervous and emotional tension within our consciousness. In this way it can be realised that music is in its essence the expression of human feelings. The language of music is the language of feeling.

But in different periods and countries people feel differently and express their feelings differently, according to the speech differences to which they are accustomed. The folk-music of any country is greatly influenced by the intonations of the language of that country. And so it comes about that a composer who desires to make his expression intelligible will use the intonations which his fellow-countrymen feel to be their own. Beethoven's musical idiom and melodic style is based upon the intonation of German and Austrian folk-music. A cultivated composer will, of course, take over some elements of the general musical culture of his day and of past periods, and integrate them into his language. Beethoven did that in many cases in the melodies and harmonies of his slow movements, which owe much to the Italian influences he absorbed through the intermediary of Haydn's and Mozart's work and of the Italian opera. His work in arranging Scottish and Irish folk-songs also inspired several of the melodies of his own instrumental compositions. But all this musical material was worked over by Beethoven and used to convey his feelings about the world of human society and of nature. He chose precisely those melodic phrases and harmonies which would, he thought, convey his beliefs in humanity and human progress, his hatred of war and oppression, his unconquerable hope in the achievement by man of the ideals of freedom, equality and fraternity.

Beethoven's language is not difficult to understand. The full appreciation of the finer technical points of his works only yield themselves, of course, to study. The more you understand of his formal and constructive methods the more you will enjoy his music. But you can appreciate it and receive its message and its inspiration without knowing all the technical details of symphonic structure. It was written for men and women to enable them to share the composer's belief in the glorious future of human society, whose vision impelled him to work for its attainment.

Beethoven was almost alone in his later years as a fighter for the cause of peace and brotherhood. We are not in that unhappy position to-day. Millions of people all over the world are fighting for peace and against those who would plunge humanity again into "accursed war" as Beethoven called it. Is not Beethoven's music therefore meant for us? Shall we not delight in its beauty, and draw strength from its power to express struggle and triumph and the joy which will attend the achievement of a new world of truly human relationships, which can only be attained by struggle, as Beethoven understood so well?

The greatness of Beethoven does not lie solely in his flow of melodic invention and his command of technical resources, but in the fact that he used his great musical gift and painfully acquired technical capacity to express in every way open to him the problems of his time, so as to bring to the men and women around him the clarity of mind and courage of heart which would enable them to take a step farther along the radiant path of human progress.

6

Opera in Tartu

Tartu is the second city of the Estonian Soviet Socialist Republic. It was founded by a Russian feudal lord, Varoslav I, in 1030 A.D. and given the Russian name Yuriev.

Estonia has suffered a terrible history of wars of conquest. In 1215 it was over-run by the Teutonic Knights, whom a popular uprising in 1223 failed to dislodge. These German barons were driven out in the 16th Century by Russian overlords, after which Russians, Poles and Swedes disputed possession of the country. In 1704 Tzar Peter the Great routed the Swedes and incorporated Estonia into the Russian Empire, thus ensuring for it 210 years of uninterrupted peace. Tartu had been re-named Dorpat by the Germans. In 1802 a university was founded there and in 1870 the Vanemuine Theatre. After the October Revolution Estonia, unlike Finland, declared itself a soviet socialist republic within the U.S.S.R. But it was at once invaded by German troops, torn from the Soviet Union and declared a bourgeois republic under the Treaty of Brest-Litovsk in March, 1918. There then followed the invasion of the Soviet Union from all sides, in which vile crime against humanity the British ruling-class, led by Mr Winston Churchill, took an eager part. As invariably happens in such cases, the aggressors won the first round, but the fourteen invading armies were all eventually defeated by the Soviet peoples by 1921, the British having gracefully retreated a year or so earlier. It is a tribute to the good sense of the Estonian people that they forced their capitalists to sign the first peace treaty of any with the Soviet Government in Dorpat in February, 1920.

Estonia was invaded by Hitler's armies in 1941 and occupied until the Nazi collapse. Concentration camps were set up and on one single day in the neighbourhood of Tartu 30,000 Estonian patriots were shot in cold blood by the Nazis and the Estonian fascists.

Since 1945 the Estonian Soviet Socialist Republic has developed an immense cultural life along national lines. Tartu was given back its original Estonian name; its present population is nearly 100,000. Every four years choral festivals in Tallinn, the capital of Estonia, and Tartu attract massed choirs of 30,000 and 8,000 singers respectively with audiences which reach 100,000 and 30,000. The University in Tartu has vastly increased in size; its neuro-pathological institute is famous and attached to it is a new geo-physical institute with a large modern observatory.

The Vanemuine Theatre occupies a new building which will shortly include a Concert-hall; it holds about 800. It gives opera, drama, ballet and operetta with its own resident ensembles. This season (1969-70) it staged my opera *The Sugar Reapers*, the prèmiére being held on November 1st. The public comes from the town, the surrounding villages and also from Tallinn, 75 miles away. It includes a high proportion of young people. During my stay in Tartu I visited one of the secondary schools and spoke to about 80 boys and girls of the three highest forms, who were learning the English language. At one point I asked those who had seen at least one opera to hold up their hands; about three-quarters did so. I also spoke to the students of the English Faculty in the University; here nearly all raised their hands. I visited a primary school in a village some 20 miles away; parties of children even from there were in the habit of visiting the theatre several times during each season.

The Estonians are highly literate. Many poets and novelists have been writing in the Estonian language for more than a hundred years. There are epics from very early times. The language has no relation to any Latin, Teutonic or Slavonic language, but immense numbers of books in other European languages have been translated. Until 1945 the main foreign language was German; since then Russian has been taught in all schools, while English is the most popular second language. I think this circumstance may have helped to pave the way to a sympathetic reception of an opera by an English librettist and composer.

Opera is certainly the most complicated form of entertainment which human society has as yet developed. From this it follows that the opera producer faces very complicated problems. It has been my lot to experience nine* different productions of my first three operas, one produced by myself, the remainder by seven other producers. Eight productions were in socialist countries and one in Britain. Somerset Maugham in *The Summing Up* wrote as follows:

> The producer is a man of ideas, but of few, and that is a disastrous thing. To conceive ideas is exhilarating, but it is only safe when you conceive so many that you ascribe no undue consequence to them and can take them for what they are worth. People who conceive few find it very difficult not to regard them with inordinate respect.

The results are often disastrous in the western world, when it is demanded of the producer in principle that he should conceive the production solely according to his own individual view-point. The wildest absurdities often result, especially with classical drama. It is true that with opera the technical difficulties of achieving musical accuracy on the stage put paid to a producer's highest flights of fancy; the result, at least under the inadequate rehearsal conditions unavoidable in Britain, is a dull level of mediocrity or, as with Schoenberg's *Moses and Aaron* at Covent Garden, mediocrity enfeebled with half-baked pornography.

My one British production, *Men of Blackmoor*, given by the Oxford University Opera Club, was in the hands of a highly intelligent producer to whom the subject and style of the work were sympathetic. The performance suffered gravely, however, from causes over which the producer had no control; the inadequacy of the stage, the low standard of orchestral playing and the poor acting by some of the principal singers. In one of the Continental productions the effect of the same opera was entirely ruined because the headstrong young woman producer, who appeared to dislike the opera, tried to make the production interesting by applying her misunderstanding of Brecht's *Kleines Organon des Theaters* to a work which demanded quite other treatment; she had indeed not few ideas but only one.

In the socialist countries a producer may quite likely be a convinced and very well-read Marxist; in the Soviet Union he or she will certainly be a profound student of Stanislavsky and may even have experienced some of his actual productions or at least productions by producers

---

* This number has now increased to twelve professional productions in ten different European opera houses and two amateur productions. (1.1.1980)

who had worked with him. This was my good fortune in the
Vanemuine Theatre, Tartu, Estonia, where the director of the theatre,
Kaarel Ird, produced *The Sugar Reapers* or *Guajaana Johnny* as the title
given to it in Leipzig appeared in the Estonian language. He was able to
co-ordinate the activities of an excellent choreographer, a brilliant
woman stage designer, an admirable choir-master, also a woman, a fine
ensemble of solo singers, choir members, dancers and orchestral players,
the whole very ably conducted indeed by the music director, Erich
Koelar. The complicated stage management was brilliantly but unobtru-
sively commanded by the stage director. Intensive rehearsals occupied
in all four weeks; on six days, including Saturdays and Sundays, in each
of three four weeks rehearsals took place on the stage, with or without
orchestra, from 11 a.m. till 3 p.m. or sometimes later, and in a large
rehearsal room from 7 till 10 p.m. The members of the ensemble were
nearly all Estonians, though a few were Russians; the pianist in the
orchestra was an Uzbek girl from Tashkent.

The first problem to be solved was that of the translation into
Estonian. This had been undertaken by a leading Estonian poet, Kulno
Suevalep. Two difficulties had arisen. Firstly, in Estonian all poly-
syllabic words, whether of two or seven syllables, bear an accent on
the first syllable; words like 'preference' abound while an intonation
like 'prefer' does not exist; this makes a translation into the Estonian
language for music extraordinarily difficult. Secondly, this
particular translator had sought constantly for poetic images for their
own sake, often at the cost of failing to put across what the character
had been given to say in the poetic but also trenchant libretto by my
wife. Many changes were made at Ird's behest, some as late as three
days before the premiere, which made the singers' task more agitating.
At one point, in an important conversation which takes place while a
samba is being danced, there seemed no possibility of an intelligible
Estonian text being fitted to my original note-values, and the singers
had been instructed to speak and not to sing. I raised an objection to
this, as there is no other point where the spoken word occurs, except
during certain radio announcements through a loud-speaker. Mr. Ird,
Mr. Koelar and I then got together; they worked out an Estonian text
quite freely, reciting it to me to enable me to mark the accents and
long vowels; I retired to my hotel bedroom and there provided a new
set of note-values to the same dance-accompaniment. The next day it
was tried out and declared an exemplary passage of Estonian musical
intonation. I only hope that it does not stick out noticeably from the

rest of the translation, but this point was never raised.

The remaining problems of production were normal to all opera productions. These are, firstly, the placing of the singer so that he or she happens at certain strategic moments to be facing the audience and, more important, the conductor, without it being apparent that this has been a matter of imaginative calculation; secondly, and far more important and difficult, the awakening in the singer's mind of the mental and emotional state of the character all the time he or she is on the stage, whether singing or not, while paying constant attention to the flow of the music in order to achieve a confident entry. In the dialogues of my operas every nuance of feeling of each character is reflected at any particular moment in the note values and orchestral accompaniment; if the singer is not inwardly reflecting the nuance of feeling the entry, even if musically accurate, will lack conviction (it goes without saying that in arias the emotion is more generally expressed than in dialogues). It is perhaps true to say that in no opera productions of the world at present except those of Walter Felsenstein in the Komische Oper, Berlin, is this conviction achieved one hundred per cent with the whole cast. In most opera houses it is achieved only in the case of the one or two solo singers who are really fine actors or actresses; the remainder of the cast sing, take up positions as instructed by the producer and wave their arms about as they have been taught to do in the opera schools. To achieve more than this is impossible without years of training and weeks of intensive rehearsal under a first-class producer. In Tartu two of the principal solo singers were very good actors while a third was the finest actor I have ever seen on the opera stage except for Chaliapin and Maria Callas, and, I would add, also Suliotis. Mr. Ird, who is generally recognised within the U.S.S.R. as one of their greatest drama and opera producers, achieved a very high standard with all members of the cast. The chorus acted splendidly and the ballet, as one would expect in the U.S.S.R., was marvellous. The entire mise-en-scène transported Guyana to the Baltic of the North in a way that was both truthful in detail and beautiful to look at; at the first rise of the curtain the effect caused many members of the reserved Estonian public to draw in their breath.

It had long been my hope and ambition to see an opera of mine staged in the Soviet Union. And when the decision was taken by Kaarel Ird to stage *The Sugar Reapers* in the Vanemuine Theatre, Tartu, I expected much but the realities far exceeded my highest hopes.

7

National character an essential ingredient
in musical art today

[Play a portion of Stockhausen's *Kontakte* : Deutsche Grammophon Gesellschaft 1388ll]

The music to which you have just been listening is a part of Karl Heinz Stockhausen's *Kontakte* for piano, percussion and electronic sounds. The whole composition lasts about 30 minutes, and I will ask you to take my word for it that it continues in much the same vein for its entire duration. One could begin it equally well at any point, and there seems no reason why it should ever come to an end. But the composer was merciful. Or perhaps either the West German Publishers or the representatives of the Deutsche Grammophon Gesellschaft, who invested their capital in its production, advised the composer that this particular length was convenient for an L.P., and furthermore that it was the maximum length which the music-director of a radio-station was likely to inflict on his circle of listeners.

Such a production as this raises a fundamental question as to the essential characteristics of a musical work of art. The great Swiss conductor and professor of mathematics, Ernest Ansermet, has put this question as follows: "Under what conditions does music emerge from sounds, or, if you wish, under what condition does the sounding event give place to a musical event?"[1]

It is, however, not only recently and not only in the case of such a work as Stockhausen's *Kontakte* that this question is relevant. Ansermet wrote (in 1961): "When we see a part of the contemporary output lauded to the skies by a small number of professionals and

1. Ansermet: *The Crisis of Contemporary Music*. Recorded Sound, No. 13. p.165.

critics, while remaining totally incomprehensible to the great mass of listeners, it is clear that our sense of music is no longer sure of itself. The crucial point of this situation lies in the fact that neither those who defend this avant-garde music nor those who reject it are able to justify their attitude by arguments that could convince everyone."[2]

In his treatise *Les fondements de la musique dans la conscience humaine* (publ. Neuchatel 1961), certainly the most elaborate treatise on the general theory of music published during the present century, Ansermet starts from the observation that "music is made, not strictly speaking with sounds, but with tonal spatial positions, which qualify sound by what is known as pitch. These various sounds, qualified by their pitch we call "notes", designated by words or letters. Notes are said to be of higher or lower pitch. Sound has no height in the outside world, that is, in real space; it has height only for the ear and for the auditory consciousness which reflects what the ear detects. Physiology teaches us that if our hearing qualifies sounds of a given frequency by *height*, this is because they are perceived at a certain level of height in the channel of our inner ear known as the cochlea. So that the qualification of sound by its height is really a purely subjective determination of sound, but one valid for all animal or human subjectivity. To the extent that all musical data are inter-subjective, music constitutes a language of universal communication."[3]

Sounds in different spatial positions are produced by air-waves with different frequencies of vibration. One tonal position differs from another by a distance to which we give the name "interval". It is a scientifically established fact that to perceive the interval of a perfect fifth is to perceive an interval with the frequency-ratio 3/2, to perceive the perfect fourth an interval with the frequency-ratio 4/3. To perceive successively a fifth and a fourth is to arrive at the octave, whose frequency-ratio is the *product* of the two foregoing ratios, i.e.

$$\frac{3 \times 4}{2 \quad 3} = \frac{12}{6} \text{ or } \frac{2}{1}.$$

The aural impression is, however, that the fourth is *added* to the fifth, and that the octave is not the product but the sum of the two intervals. This phenomenon is explicable, Ansermet maintains, solely on the assumption that what is perceived is not the frequency-ratios of the two intervals but the logarithms of these ratios. In this way and in no other way can the product of two numbers create the effect in the auditory consciousness of their sum. The perception

2. Ibid, p.165.
3. Elid., p.165.

of these logarithms in the cochlea results in something which does not arise in nature any more than the height of a sound exists in nature: namely an interval between two tonal cochlea positions. This interval is brought about by a rise or fall in the cochlea, a rectilinear distance, endowed with a certain angle of inclination. This movement in the cochlea is accompanied by a rise or fall in affective tension within the consciousness of the percipient. A Hungarian scientist living in the U.S.A., Mr. von Bekesy, has proved by experiment that a pure sound — that is, one devoid of harmonics — excites in the ear not only the cochlear position corresponding to its frequency but also the cochlear positions corresponding to its first five harmonics. This fact proves that the human ear translates into inner tensions the intervals corresponding with the basic intervallic relations of the harmonic series. Thus the imaginary space into which music introduces us is a *structured* space, and it is structured by a system of logarithms which has its source in consciousness. Its structures are perspectives of octaves articulated at the fifth. From this octave articulated at the fifth proceeds a hierarchy of intervals to which we give the name tonality, within the network of whose relations the tensions of the composer are communicated to the listener.

To sum up, Ansermet states his basic conclusion as follows: "Music is thus a sensation of feeling. But it would be wrong to say that it is an expression of feeling, which would leave the impression that it expressed feelings we know in life. Now, the feeling lived in music is never anything but tonal feeling. But, as we have just seen, this feeling is made up of elementary affective tensions which must constitute the texture of the feelings which we know in life. So this tonal or musical feeling bears the same stamp as the feelings we know in life, and this is why, to a certain degree, we can recognise in them certain modalities of feeling (joy, sorrow, etc.,) that we already experienced in life . . . . . . Music is not, then, strictly speaking, an expression of feelings, but an expression of *man* by his modalities of feeling, for, according to the structural elements, according to the course taken by the melody, of the harmonic and rhythmic structures, that is to say, according to the way active or passive tensions become organised in tonal structures, music gives rise to the different modalities of our affective life."[4]

It follows from this that a concatenation of sounds which follow upon one another melodically or are sounded simultaneously without

4. Ibid., p.172.

regard either in principle or by accident to the basic tonal relations spaced out within the cochlea, cannot result in a musical work, in an expression of man by his modalities of feeling. Ansermet ended the lecture from which I have taken the above excerpts in the following unequivocal manner: "Between tonal and atonal music there is an impassable gulf, and if the musical world, won over by the propaganda made for it, opts decisively for atonal music, dodecaphonic or otherwise, it will lose its sense of music."[5]

Ansermet's exposition of the structured movements of the cochlea and their correspondence with the rise and fall in affective tension within consciousness establishes incontrovertibly that the structured hierarchy of intervals to which we give the name tonality is one of the essential ingredients of all sounding events which are works of musical art. There is, however, one proposition which he makes which seems to me to be unfounded, namely that the feelings lived in music are not the feelings we know in life. This proclamation that there exist such phenomena in consciousness as tonal feelings, to use Ansermet's own expression, appears to me to be unacceptable. It might be a possibility if we were to believe that consciousness functions in water-tight compartments, or might in any conditions approaching normality so function; but this is a totally unacceptable assumption. It is much simpler to admit the possibility that a rise and fall in tension such as could be experienced in life as a whole could also be expressed in musical structures.

There is one further point with which I disagree in Ansermet's general analysis. It assumes that the faculty of experiencing tonal feeling and communicating it to others arises and develops in the individual human being not only independently of all other feelings but is inborn solely as a result of heredity. There is no reason to believe, according to Ansermet, that the historical epoch during which an individual is born, his nationality, social position or general cultural background have *necessarily and inevitably* any essential parts to play in the development of his faculty of experiencing tonal feelings or communicating it to others. Greatly as I admire Ansermet's insight and analytical powers in the domain of fundamental musical theory and firmly as I agree with his conclusions concerning tonality, I find his belief in the untouchability of the faculty of tonal feeling by the impact of the surrounding world without foundation. It arises from his

5. Ibid., p.175.

general world-outlook, which informs his theory of the ways in which historical events influence musical development and change, which in my opinion also lacks any scientific basis, and it renders incomplete his analysis of the essential ingredients of all to-day's sounding events which are works of musical art. I shall return to these two points later.

The two points established in Ansermet's exposition, firstly, that music is built upon a structured hierarchy of intervals, present in the harmonic series, and secondly that its melodic, harmonic and rhythmic movement is intimately connected in some way with a rise and fall of tension in human consciousness, have been subjects of musical theory throughout European history since the fifth century B.C. They are no doubt subjects also of Chinese and Indian musical theory, the beginnings of which are said respectively to date from the fourth and fifth millennia B.C. In classical Greek and early Christian theory the structure of scales had been established, and it was believed that music had the power to affect the human soul for good or evil, in Greece in regard to social conformism, in the Christian world in a religious sense. How this occurred was not explained; whether the principles of good and evil or the feelings of ordinary life could form the actual content of music was not discussed. The effect of music was described in therapeutic terms, as nowadays the sound of some types of music is stated to have beneficial results in certain cases on people who are mentally disturbed.

Throughout the Middle Ages musical theorists were occupied exclusively with such problems as notation, the treatment of consonance and dissonance and the possibility of combining voice-parts with independent note values. As all music except for dance music was vocal, expression was already present through the words, and the question of how feeling could be expressed in instrumental music could hardly arise. This happened probably for the first time in Glarean's *Dodecachordon* (1547), when he wrote of Josquin des Prés: "No one has more effectively expressed the passions of the soul in music than this symphonist." From this time on till the year 1854 theoreticians of music and composers believed as a matter of course that the content of music was human feeling. Zarlino in his *Institutioni armoniche* of 1558 wrote: "For if in speech whether by way of narrative or imitation, matters may be treated that are joyful or mournful, and grave or without gravity, and again modest or lascivious, we must also make a choice of a harmony and a rhythm similar to the nature of the matters contained in the speech in order that in the combinations of these things, put together with proportion, may result a melody suited to the purpose."[6] And again: "In the same way, if any word expresses complaint, grief, affliction, sighs, tears and other things of this sort the harmony will be full of sadness."[7] In Rameau's *Traite de l'Harmonie* of 1722, we read: "There are harmonies that are sad, languishing, tender, agreeable, gay and striking; there are also certain successions of harmonies for the expressions of these passions."[8] This belief has persisted in the minds of the vast majority of composers and theoreticians up to the present. Thus Paul Hindemith in *The Composer's World*, written in 1951 at the age of 56, described music as "a form of communication between the author and consumer of his music"[9] and after careful analysis reached the clear proposition that "the reactions music evokes are not feelings but they are the images, memories of feelings."[10] Hindemith in *The Craft of Musical Composition* (1934) had already provided the complete detailed exposition of the structured hierarchy of intervals to which we give the name tonality. Arnold Schoenberg, despite his negation in principle of tonality, wrote in 1947, when over 70 years of age: "Music speaks in its own language of purely musical matters — or perhaps, as most aestheticians believe, of matters of feeling and fantasy."[11] This confused "perhaps" suggests that alongside the tonal feeling of Ansermet music also expresses feelings which we know in life, whereas Ansermet does not allow any alternative to tonal feeling as the content of music. Apart from this it is hardly necessary to recall that Ansermet regards Schoenberg's method of composing with twelve tones, which are related only to one another, as precluding the possibility that musical art could result, the structures so built bearing merely the semblance of music lacking as they do that tonal feeling which, in his belief, is music's essence.

In 1959 Deryck Cooke published his important treatise *The Language of Music*. The content of music is in Deryck Cooke's view "the composer's original emotional experience".[12] This experience is

6. Strunk: *Science Readings in Musical History* (Faber & Faber, 1952) pp. 256/7.
7. Ibid., pp. 256/7.
8. Ibid., pp. 572/3.
9. Paul Hindemith: *The Composer's World*. (OUP 1952) p.38.
10. Ibid., p.38.
11. Schoenberg: *Style & Idea* (London 1951) p.209.
12. Cooke: *The Language of Music* (OUP 1959) p.201.

communicated through certain basic melodic patterns within the framework of tonality wherein particular intervals or groups of intervals, rising or falling, express particular feelings; these have been used persistently throughout our musical history. Musical sensibility in the hearer means the ability to transform music into feeling.

It is significant that Ansermet arrived at the same conclusion. He wrote: "Thus, musical intervals carry precise psychic musical meanings which they derive from their musical genesis, in the same way as the words we use carry meanings derived from their genesis in language. This is why all musicians use the same intervals to signify the same affective tensions, and this is why the listener attaches the same significance to the intervals perceived as that given to it by the composer."[13]

Yet before the exposition in 1961 by Ansermet of the structured movements of cochlea, accompanied by a rise or fall in affective tension within consciousness and their correspondence with the structured space of tonality, there had never been any explanation of how the combination of air-waves of varying frequencies, sent forth by some sounding source, and which are the physical envelopes of musical works, could possibly have as their content human feeling, whether the tonal feeling that Ansermet proclaims as indispensible, or Schoenberg hints at as one possibility, or the human feelings which we know in life. Neither Zarlino in the 16th nor Hindemith in the 20th century gives any explanation of how this comes about.

In these circumstances it is not surprising that a theory so weakly supported from a scientific point of view until the year 1961, should have been disputed. This occurred in 1854, when the Viennese musicologist Eduard Hanslick, published his treatise *Vom Musikalisch-Schoenen.* The basic proposition of this work is stated as follows: "The crude material which the composer has to fashion, the vast profusion of which it is impossible fully to estimate, is the entire scale of musical notes and their inherent adaptability to an endless variety of melodies, harmonies and rhythms . . . To the question — what is to be expressed with all this material? The answer will be: musical ideas. Now a musical idea is an end in itself and not a means for representing feelings and thoughts."[14] Hanslick does not attempt to prove this proposition but states as it as an axiom. It might be assumed that he is as equally unjustified as those who assume human

13. Ansermet: *Crisis of Contemporary Music,* p.172.
14. Hanslick: *The Beautiful in Music* (Novello, 1891) pp. 66/7.

feelings in music without being able to prove their existence. But as a matter of scientific correctness this is not so. He proceeds from the material of music, air-waves, which impinge upon the ear and refrains from drawing further conclusions about their content. It is up to those of us who believe that what music expresses is something other than music to supply the proof. (It is the same in theology. It is not up to the atheists to prove that there is no God, but to the deists to prove that they are justified in believing that there is one.)

Hanslick's attack on the notion that music expresses human feelings had no apparent result on composers or other musicians until after the First World War. Since then it has found one eminent and at least one not so eminent supporter among the composers of today. Igor Stravinsky has on two occasions denied content to music. In his Autobiography of 1935 he wrote: "Music is by its very nature powerless to express anything at all, whether a feeling, an attitude of mind, a psychological mood, a phenomenon of nature."[15] Thirteen years later in 1948 when 66 years old he restated this proposition as follows: "Do we not, in truth, ask the impossible of music, when we expect it to express feelings, to translate dramatic situations, even to imitate nature?"[16] Like Hanslick, he makes no attempt to justify this assertion, but states it as an axiom. Positively Stravinsky defines music as "a form of speculation in terms of sound and time . . . music is what unifies . . . music comes to reveal itself as a form of communion with our fellow man and with the Supreme Being."[17] This incursion of theology into musicology cannot be accepted as scientific.

More recently the American composer John Cage entered the lists in support of a variation of Hanslick's theory. In 1957 he wrote as follows: "Tones must be allowed to be tones. They must no longer carry an idea or an association or whatever."[18] Mr. Cage provides no explanation of why the year 1957 is to be acknowledged as a sort of nodal point of time, after which a new demand is required from music. Music, he implies, carried an extra-musical content in the past, but it must do so no longer. (This formulation would have been totally unacceptable to Hanslick, whose theory is that music cannot be and never has been a means for carrying "an idea or an association or whatever".) In the history of musical theory there can have been few

15. Stravinsky: *Chroniques de ma Vie* (Paris, 1935) p.83.
16. Stravinsky: *The Poetics of Music* (OUP 1948) pp.139-142.
17. Ibid., pp.139-142.
18. John Cage: *Silence*.

propositions of a more staggering absurdity than this one by Mr. Cage.

Yet the theory of Hanslick as formulated by him cannot be considered to be defeated merely because his present-day followers present it in unconvincing formulations, either the dogmatic reiteration with theological overtones of Igor Stravinsky or the fatuous inanity of John Cage. There is, however, an approach to the problem from a totally different angle, no less fundamental than that of Ansermet, but one from which we are enabled to crown the edifice on which he has so magisterially enthroned the principle of tonality. It approaches the problem, not from a consideration of the cochlea alone but of man and woman as music-maker, whether creator or performer, in a more general physiological sense and as a member of some form of human social organisation. Ansermet's method is to study an activity which takes place within an individual, while at the same time placing the individual in the quite impossible situation of total isolation and keeping him there. This is in fact the phenomenological method of Edmund Husserl, which Ansermet with due acknowledgement applies to the phenomenon Music. Useful as the method has proved within certain circumscribed limits and astonishing as have been at times its implications, as for example with Jean-Paul Sartre in the domain of ethics, it can lead to misleading conclusions, when it is not corrected by references to more broadly based facts of human life.

The simple proposition from which this approach starts is the following: musical art would not exist if human beings did not possess ears and voices. (I put ears first because among our vertebrate ancestors are some who possess ears but not voices.) This is one of those very few self-evident propositions which require no proof. But it is supported by the facts of musical history. Kurt Sachs wrote in *The Rise of Music in the Ancient World*: "Music began with singing. However rudimentary this singing may be, it flows all through primitive man's life. It conveys his poetry, and in rest and peaceful work diverts, elates and lulls; it gives hypnotic trance to those who heal the sick and strive for luck and life in magic incantation, it keeps awake the dancers' yielding muscles, intoxicates the fighting men and leads the squaw to ecstacy."[19] Returning to this self-evident proposition that music exists because man has ears and a voice, we note a peculiarity of this physical organ, the voice. When we use our voices the tones rise and fall in pitch and fluctuate in volume according to whether we are in a greater or lesser

19. Kurt Sachs: *The Rise of Music in the Ancient World* (Dent 1944) pp.21/22.

condition of excitement. The reason for this is that in moments of greater excitement our muscular tension increases, bringing about involuntarily the parting and consequent stretching of the vocal cords. Furthermore, the more rapid expulsion of air from the lungs meeting the vocal cords can cause a rise in pitch similar to that brought about on other wind instruments. (The involuntary use of the voice is here described; in moments of controlled excitement it is possible to utter intensely emotionally charged words in a low, whispered tone.) Music, whether vocal or instrumental, consists of successions of tones of varying degrees of pitch, volume and duration. It is thus nothing other than a reflection of greater or lesser degrees of tension in the human organism, a reflection in very truth of human feeling. (Instrumental music, which began in all cases as a representation of vocal music, is nothing other than this in its essential nature.) Therewith the theory that music is the expression in sound of human feeling receives an invincible foundation.

It is evident that the greater or lesser degrees of tension which accompany vocal sounds of higher or lower pitch link up with the movements of rise and fall in the cochlea. There is thus no contradiction between the result arrived at from the starting-poing of this self-evident proposition and the findings of Ansermet's enquiry, except in regard to those two of his conclusions, against which I raised objections earlier in this paper: one, as the content of music it substitutes instead of Ansermet's postulated tonal feeling the feelings we know in life; and two, as the human subject it substitutes, instead of the general human individual whose musical faculty is derived from his heredity and develops untouched by historical or social experiences, the concrete human individual whose brain is certainly hereditarily acquired but whose consciousness is incessantly besieged from birth by the impact of social events and the influences of whatever cultural heritage happen to surround him. This method of approach thus provides a scientifically based solution to the two points of Ansermet's analysis which rest, in my opinion, upon unacceptable assumptions.

It remains for me to draw a final conclusion from the position we have reached. Music began with singing. The original functions of music enumerated by Kurt Sachs (who however omitted the vitally important work-song as a genre) are still being fulfilled, but alongside of these functions musical works of.art have been created which express in highly developed musical forms "man by his modalities of feeling," to quote again from Ansermet. These musical works, whether with or without words, are directed to a public of listeners, and through them the composer communicates his or her feelings, whether these be associated with abstract ideas or aroused by some event or recollection of some past event, experienced directly or by hearsay. Each individual's faculty of self-expression is developed within a particular national and cultural framework. When he expresses himself in words, he does so, unless artificially required or conditioned to do otherwise, in his own language with its particular metrical accentuation, tempo, rise and fall; and this verbal vocal expression is accompanied by gestures, which differ very markedly between people of different nationalities. Music, which began with singing, develops from the start its turns of melody, peculiarities of rhythm and accentuation which are brought about by its association with the words of whatever language is being sung; and instrumental music, as has been already pointed out, is nothing other essentially than a technically elaborated representation of vocal music. From this it follows that a composer, if he is to express himself truthfully and without yielding to the pressures of fashion or without being deceived by superficial and false theorising about the necessity of internationalism in art in the present technological age, will do so within the framework of musical turns of phrase which have resulted from the basic vocal music of his own nationality. This theory of "intonation" as an essential ingredient of musical art was first propouned by the Russian musicologist Boris Asafiev in 1930 in his treatise *Musical Form as Process*.[20] There is no scientific basis whatever for the argument that whereas a literary artist should develop along the lines of his national tradition and not write as much like a foreigner as possible, in music, the art built up from its very inception upon the melodic and rhythmic basis of language, the composer should deny this cultural heritage in principle. By doing so the delicate processes of the creative faculty within his consciousness will be isolated and artificially shielded from any active relationship with the rest of his conscious thinking and feeling, so that his musical creations will be in a sense translations and therefore to some extent distorted versions of what he wishes to communicate. (This situation only obtains so long as human society is organised in national groupings. At some future date unforeseeably remote this may no longer be so; but my paper is not speculative but only concerned with the conditions of the present.) It is not

20. B. V. Asafiev: *Musikalnaza Forma kak Progess*. (Leningrad. 1963).

to be expected that Ansermet, in his warning about the danger to the future of musical art from atonal music, dodecaphonic or otherwise, raised this aspect of national or non-national style; the above-mentioned danger of contradiction within the creative musical faculty does not exist for him, since he argues that this faculty exists a *priori* in a condition shielded from the feelings we know in life and that the composer *as such* has no fundamental bias towards his national cultural heritage.

In saying this, I do not wish, however, in any way to diminish the admiration in which I hold the work of Ernest Ansermet in his marshalling of the unchallengeable arguments for tonality as an essential ingredient of musical art. Supplemented in the ways I have just outlined, namely, by the anthropological and sociological approach to the creative aspects of music instead of that of phenomenology, they provide a scientifically based general theory of music on which the achievements of composers and the evaluation of their works by music critics can be firmly founded.

Complete list of works

STAGE WORKS

(a) Operas

Wat Tyler　　Opera in Two Acts with Prologue
　Libretto by Nancy Bush
　　No opus number　　　　1948-51　　　Henschelverlag, Berlin
　　　　　　　　　　　　　　　　　　　　Novello, London

Men of Blackmoor　　Opera in Two Acts
　Libretto by Nancy Bush
　　No opus number　　　　1954-55　　　Henschelverlag, Berlin
　　　　　　　　　　　　　　　　　　　　Stainer & Bell, London

The Sugar Reapers　　Opera in Two Acts
　Libretto by Nancy Bush
　　No opus number　　　　1961-63　　　Henschelverlag, Berlin

Joe Hill: The Man Who Never Died　　Opera in Two Acts
　Libretto by Barrie Stavis
　　No opus number　　　　1966-68　　　MS

The Press Gang (or The Escap'd Apprentice)　　Children's Opera
　Libretto by Nancy Bush
　　No opus number　　　　1946　　　　W.M.A., London

The Spell Unbound　　Opera for girls in an Elizabethan setting
　Libretto by Nancy Bush
　　No opus number　　　　1953　　　　Novello, London

The Ferryman's Daughter　　An Opera of the Thames Waterside for
　　　　　　　　　　　　　　　　Schools
　Libretto by Nancy Bush
　　No opus number　　　　1961　　　　Novello, London

(b) Ballets
His War or Yours   1935
Mining   1935
Men and Machines   1934 (in 'Pageant of Labour')

(c) Incidental Music for Theatre
The Pageant of Labour   1934   MS
The Pageant of Co-operation 1938   MS
The Star Turns Red (O'Casey)   1940   MS
The Duke In Darkness (Patrick Hamilton)   1942   MS
Macbeth   1947   MS
Communist Manifesto Centenary Pageant   1948   MS

CHORAL WORKS

Song To The Men of England (Text: Shelley)
   Unaccompanied Mixed Chorus
   No opus number   1929   Stainer & Bell
The Road (Text: Violet A. Friedlander)
   Unaccompanied Mixed Chorus
   No opus number   1929   Stainer & Bell
Britain's Part (Text: Alan Bush)
   Mixed Chorus, Speaker, Piano, Percussion
   No opus number   1943   MS
The Winter Journey (Text: Randall Swingler)
   Cantata for Soprano & Baritone Soli,
   Mixed Chorus, String Quintet, Harp
   Opus 29   1946   Stainer & Bell
Lidice (Text: Nancy Bush)
   Unaccompanied Mixed Chorus
   No opus number   1947   Workers' Music Association
Song Of Friendship (Text: Nancy Bush)
   Cantata for Bass Solo, Mixed Chorus and orchestra
   Opus 34   1949   MS
The Dream Of Llewelyn Ap Gruffydd (Text: Randall Swingler)
   Male voice Chorus and Piano
   Opus 35   1950   MS
The Ballad of Freedom's Soldier (Text: John Manifold)
   Tenor and Bass-baritone soli, Mixed Chorus and Orchestra
   Opus 44   1953   MS

Like Rivers Flowing (Text: Nancy Bush)
    Part song for S.S.A.T.B.
    No opus number   1957   Stainer & Bell
Nicht Den Tod Aus Der Ferne (Text: Armin Mueller)
    Baritone Solo and Mixed Unison Chorus accompaniment for
    Clarinet, Trumpet, Percussion and Piano
    No opus number   1958   MS
Ballade Vom Marsch Auf Aldermaston (Text: Armin Mueller)
    (English version, text: Nancy Bush)
    Speaker, Mixed Chorus, accompaniment for 2 Horns, 2 Trumpets,
    2 Guitars, Percussion and Double-bass.
    No opus number   1958   MS
The World Is His Song (Text: Nancy Bush)
    Mezzo-Soprano or Baritone Solo and Mixed Chorus, accompaniment
    for 2 Horns, 2 Trumpets, 3 Trombones, Tuba, Guitar, Percussion
    and Piano
    Opus 51   1958   MS
The Tide That Will Never Turn, Declaration by Hugh McDiarmid
    Two Speakers, Bass (or Baritone) Solo, Mixed Chorus, Strings,
    Percussion and Piano
    No opus number   1961   MS
During Music (Text: Dante Gabriel Rossetti)
    Unaccompanied Part-Song (S.A.T.B.)
    No opus number   1963   Novello
The Alps and Andes of The Living World (Text by Shakespeare, T.H.
    Huxley and Nancy Bush)
    Cantata for Speaker, Tenor solo and Mixed Chorus with orchestral
    accompaniment.
    Opus 66   1968   MS
Songs of Asian Struggle arranged by Alan Bush
    Polishing the Gun: song of the Malayan partisans: The Rice Harvest:
    song from North Korea: My Country in Captivity: song of the Huk
    partisans of the Phillipine Islands: The Jacket-makers' Song: song
    from North Vietnam: Chinese Students' Song: song against the
    Japanese invaders of the 1930's.
                    1969   MS
Men Of Felling (Text by Nancy Bush)
    Male Voice Choir with Piano,
    Opus 72   1971   MS

Earth Has Grain To Grow (Text: by C. Day Lewis)
   Mixed Chorus unaccompanied.
                    1972   Novello
Carol: The Earth Awaking (Text by Nancy Bush)
   For Female Choir with Organ.
      Opus 74   1972   MS
Song For Angela Davis (Text by Nancy Bush)
   Mixed Chorus unaccompanied or with piano accompaniment.
                    1972   MS
Africa Is My Name (Text by Nancy Bush)
   Mezzo-Soprano Solo, Mixed Chorus and Piano (or Orchestra)
      Opus 85   1976   MS

Songs For mixed Voice Chorus with Piano Accompaniment
Published by the Workers' Music Association
Song To Labour (Text: Charlotte Perkin Gilman)   1926
Question And Answer (Text: Roy Atterbury)   1931
Hunger Marchers' Song (Text: Randall Swingler)   1934
Labour's Song Of Challenge (Text: Randall Swingler)   1936
Make Your Meaning Clear (Text: Randall Swingler)   1939
Against The People's Enemies (Text: Randall Swingler)   1940
March of The Workers (Text: William Morris)   1940
The Ice Breaks (Text: Randall Swingler)   1940
Truth On The March (Text: Randall Swingler)   1940
Unite And Be Free (Text: Alan Bush)   1941
The Great Red Army (Text: Randall Swingler)   1942
Song Of The Commons Of England (Text: Miles Carpenter) 1942
A World For Living (Text: Randall Swingler)   1946
Our Song (Text: Nancy Bush)   1948
Shining Vision (Text: Montagu Slater)   1950
Song Of The Cosmonaut (Text: Miles Tomalin)   1961

Two-Part Songs
Published by the Workers' Music Association
The Ice Breaks (Text: Randall Swingler)
The Great Red Army (Text: Randall Swingler)
Till Right Is Done (Text: Will Saknow)

Songs
Two Songs for Soprano & Chamber Orchestra (Text: H. Monro)
   Orchestra: 1.1.1.1.2 Horns, Harp, Strings
      Opus 7   1925   MS

Songs Of The Doomed (Text: F.C. Boden)
    Song Cycle for Tenor, with Female Chorus and Piano
    Opus 14   1929   MS

Prison Cycle (Text: Ernst Toller)
    Baritone and Piano
    No opus number   1939   MS
    (in collaboration with Alan Rawsthorne)

Toulon (Text: Nancy Bush)
    Messo-Soprano, with Mixed Chorus and Piano
    No opus number   1942   MS

Voices Of The Prophets (Texts: Isaiah, Milton, Blake and Blackman)
    Cantata for Tenor Voice and Piano
    Opus 41   1953   Stainer & Bell
    1. From the Sixty-fifth chapter of the book of the Prophet Isaiah
    2. From the Oration 'Against the Scholastic Philosophy' by John Milton
    3. From 'Selections from Milton' by William Blake
    4. From 'My Song for all Men' by Peter Blackman

Seafarers' Songs for Baritone and Piano (Texts: Penguin Book of English Folksongs)
    The Ship in Distress: Ratcliffe Highway: The Greenland Whale Fishery: Jack the Jolly Tar
    Opus 57   1961   MS

The Freight Of Harvest (poems by Sylvia Townsend Warner)
    Song-cycle for Tenor and Piano
    Country Thought from a Town; The Sailor; The Maiden; The Load of Fern.
    Opus 69   1969   MS

Life's Span, Song Cycle for Mezzo-Soprano and Piano
    A Child Asleep (Nancy Bush); Learning to Talk (C. Day Lewis); The Long Noonday (Nancy Bush); Beauty's End is in Sight (C. Day Lewis)
    Opus 77   1974   MS

De Plenos Poderes, poems by Pablo Neruda
    Song-cycle for Baritone and Piano
    El Pueblo; Nada Mas; El Perezoso
    Opus 86   1977   MS

Woman's Life (Poems by Nancy Bush)
    Song-cycle for Soprano and Piano.
    Prologue; Weaving Song; Factory Day; Epilogue

Opus 87   1977   MS
Two Shakespeare Sonnets for Baritone in a setting for Chamber
  Orchestra
Opus 91   1980   MS

ORCHESTRAL WORKS

Symphonic Impression
  Opus 8   1926-27   MS
Dance Overture
  Opus 12   1935   Stainer & Bell
  Orchestra: 3232 — Alto and tenor Saxs, 4331 — Timp. Perc. Strings
  (Original version for Military Band, 1930)
Concerto For Piano And Orchestra
  Baritone Solo and Male Voice Chorus in last movement
  (Text: Randall Swingler)
  Orchestra: 333 — 4331 — Timp. Perc. Harp. Strings
  Opus 18   1937   Stainer & Bell
Symphony No. 1 in C
  Orchestra: 2233 — 4 Horns, 3 Cornets, 3 Trombones, Tuba, Timp.
  Perc. Harp, Piano, Strings
  Opus 21   1939-40   Stainer & Bell
Meditation On A German Song On 1848
  Solo Violin and String Orchestra
  Opus 22   1941   MS
Overture: Festal Day (Original title: Birthday Greeting in Honour of
  Vaughan Williams)
  Orchestra: 1122 — 2210 — Piano, Perc. Strings
  Opus 23   1942   MS
Fantasia On Soviet Themes
  Orchestra: 2222 — 4231 — Timp, Perc, Strings
  Opus 24   1942   Novello
Overture 'Resolution'
  Orchestra: 2222 — 4230 — Timp. Perc. Piano, Strings
  Opus 25   1946   MS
Homage To William Sterndale Bennett
  String Orchestra
  Opus 27   1946   MS
English Suite
  String Orchestra
  Opus 28   1945-46   MS

Piers Plowman's Day (Symphonic Suite)
    Orchestra: 2222 — 4230 — Perc. Timp. Strings
    Opus 30   1946-47   Joseph Williams

Concerto for Violin and Orchestra
    Orchestra: 2222 — 4330 — Timp. Perc. Strings
    Opus 32   1948   MS

Symphony No 2: The Nottingham
    Orchestra: 2222 — 4331 — Timps. Perc. Strings
    Opus 33   1949   Stainer & Bell

Concert Suite for Cello and Orchestra
    1. Introduction and Divisions on a Ground 2. Ballet
    3. Poem 4. Dance
    Orchestra: 2222 — 4230 — Timp. perc. Harp. Strings
    Opus 37   1952   MS

Defender Of Peace: Character Portrait for Orchestra
    Orchestra: 2222 — 4331 — Timp. Perc. Piano Strings
    Opus 39   1952   Soviet Music Publishers, Moscow

Dorian Passacaglia and Fugue for Orchestra
    Orchestra: 2222 D.Bs optional — 4331 Timp. Perc. Strings
    Opus 52   1959   Novello

Symphony No 3: The Byron Symphony
    With Baritone Solo and Mixed Chorus in last movement (Text: D.
    Solomos)
    Orchestra: 3333 — 4431 — Harp. Timp. Perc. Strings
    Opus 53   1959-60   MS

For A Festal Occasion for Organ and Orchestra
    Orchestra: 2222 — 4230 — Timp. Perc. optional Strings
    Opus 58   1961   MS
    (Version of Opus 56 No. 2)

Variations, Nocturne and Finale on an English Sea-Song for Pianoforte
   and Orchestra
    Orchestra: 2222 — 4231 — Timp. Perc (2 players) Strings
    Opus 60   1962   Novello

Partita Concertante for Orchestra
    Overture; Hornpipe; Air; Cheviot Reel
    Orchestra: 2.1.2.1. — 2.2.1 — Timp. Perc (2 players) Strings
    Opus 63   1965   Novello

Time Remembered, a Piece for Chamber Orchestra.
    Opus 67   1969   MS

Scherzo For Wind Orchestra with Percusion
    Opus 68   1969   Nóvello
Africa: symphonic movement for Piano and Orchestra,
    Opus 73   1972   Peters
Concert Overture for An Occasion
    Opus 74   1972   MS
The Liverpool Overture
    Opus 76   1973   MS
Festival March For British Youth
    Opus 78   1973   MS

WORKS FOR WIND BAND

Pavane For The Castleton Queen for Brass Band

Solo Cornet (B flat)	1st Baritone in B flat
Sop. Cornet (E flat)	2nd Baritone in B flat
Rep. Cornet (B flat)	1st & 2nd Trombone in B flat
& Fl.	Bass Trombone
2nd Cornet (B flat)	Euphonium in B flat
3rd Cornet (B flat)	E flat Bass
Solo, 1st & 2nd	Drums
Horn in E flat	

    Opus 43   1953   MS
Dance Overture for Military Band
    Opus 12   1930   MS
Russian Glory for Military Band (March on Soviet Songs)
    No opus number   1941   MS (with B.B.C.)

CHAMBER MUSIC AND INSTRUMENTAL SOLOS

Three Pieces For Two Pianos
    Opus 1   1921   Chappell
Sonata in B Minor for Piano
    Opus 2   1921   Chappell
Fantasy for Violin & Piano
    Opus 3   1923   MS
String Quartet in A Minor
    Opus 4   1923   Stainer & Bell
Quartet for Piano, Violin, Viola & Cello
    Opus 5   1924   MS
Five Pieces for Violin, Viola, Cello, Clarinet & Horn
    Opus 6   1925   MS

Prelude And Fugue for Piano
    Opus 9   1927   Oxford Univ. Press
Relinquishment for Piano
    Opus 11   1928   Oxford Univ. Press
Dialectic for String Quartet
    Opus 15   1929   MS
Concert Piece for Cello & Piano
    Opus 17   1936   MS
Meditation On A German Song Of 1848 for Violin & Piano
    Opus 22   1941   MS
Le Quartorze Juillet: Esquisse for Piano
    Opus 38   1943   Stainer & Bell
Lyric Interlude for Violin Solo with Piano accompaniment
    Opus 26   1944   MS
Three Concert Studies for Piano, Violin & Cello
    Opus 31   1947   Novello
Times Of Day. Four Piano Pieces for Children
    No opus number   1950   MS
Trent's Broad Reaches for Horn and Piano
    Opus number 36 1951   Schott
Two Easy Pieces for Cello & Piano
    1. Song Across the Water, 2. Fireside Story.
    No opus number   1951   Stainer & Bell
Borodine: Mazurka, arranged for Piano Duet (Workers' Music Assoc.)
Three English Song Preludes for Organ.
    Opus 40   1952   Oxford University Press
Northumbrian Impressions: for Northumbrian Small Pipes
    1. Prelude. 2. Lament. 3. Dance.
    Opus 42   1953   MS
Northumbrian Impressions: Version for Oboe & Piano
    Opus 42a   1953   Novello
Autumn Poem for Horn & Piano
    Opus 45   1954   Schott
Nocturne for Pianoforte Solo
    Opus 46   1957   Novello
Two Melodies for Viola with Piano accompaniment
    1. Song Melody. 2. Dance Melody.
    Opus 47   1957   Joseph Williams
Mister Playford's Tunes: a little Suite for Piano
    1. Argeers. 2. The Whish and Peppers Black. 3. Nonesuch. 4. The

Beggar Boy. 5. The Slip, a Going-out.

Opus 49   1958   MS

Two Ballads Of The Sea for Piano

  1. The Cruel Sea Captain. 2. Reuben Ranzo

Opus 50   1957-58   Stainer & Bell

Suite For Harpsichord or Piano

  1. Pavan. 2. Galiard. 3. Air. 4. Longway Set.

Opus 54   1960   Peters Edition

Three African Sketches for Flute with piano accompaniment.

  1. Southern Rhodesia. 2. Zululand. 3. Congo.

Opus 55   1960   Peters Edition

Two Occasional Pieces for Organ

  1. For a solemn occasion. 2. For a festal occasion (also arranged for Organ and Orchestra).

Opus 56   1960   Novello

Three Raga Melodies for Unaccompanied Solo Violin

  1. Himavirdani Raga. 2. Nadatha-Rangini Raga. 3. Garudavirdani Raga.

Opus 59   1961   MS

Prelude, Air and Dance for Solo Violin, String Quartet and Percussion

Opus 61   1963-64   Novello

Meditation On The Ballad Geordie for Double Bass and Piano

Opus 62   1964   MS

Two Dances for Cimbalom

Opus 64   1965   Editio Murica, Budapest

Suite for Two Pianos

  Prologue; Volga Harvest; Kirloch Iorram; Samarkand Drigolch; Pennine Round.

Opus 65   1967   MS

Serenade For String Quartet

Opus 70   1969   MS

Pianoforte Sonata in A flat

Opus 71   1970   MS

Corentyne Kwe-Kwe for Piano Solo

Opus 75   1972   MS

Letter Galiard for Piano Solo

Opus 79   1974   MS

Suite Of Six for String Quartet

Opus 81   1975   MS

Sonatina For Recorders And Piano
Opus 82   1975   MS
Compass Points, Suite for Pipes
Opus 83   1976   MS
Twenty-Four Preludes for Piano
Opus 86   1977   MS
Sonatina For Viola And Piano
Opus 88   1978   Schauer
Pro Pace Et Felicitate Generis Humani, Rhapsody for Cello & Piano
Opus 89   1979   MS
Souvenir D'une Nuit D'été après Sergei Liapunov, for piano
Opus 90   1979   MS

Productions and broadcasts of the four full-length operas

Wat Tyler
(Subject: the English Peasant Rebellion of 1381)
Arts Council of Great Britain Prize in Festival of Britain Opera
    Competition   1951
Radio Version — Berliner Rundfunk   1952
Production — Leipzig Opera House (world première)   1953
Production — Rostock Opera House   1955
Radio Version — B.B.C.   1956
Production — Magdeburg Opera House   1959
Production — Sadlers' Wells Theatre, London   1974

Men Of Blackmoor
(Subject: the struggle of the Northumbrian Coal Miners, early 19th
    Century)
Production — German National Theatre, Weimar (world première)
                                                            1956
Production — Jena Opera House   1957
Radio Version — Radio DDR   1958
Production — Leipzig Opera House   1959
Production — Zwickau Opera House   1960
Production — Oxford University Opera Club   1960
Radio Version — B.B.C.   1965
Production — Bristol University Opera Society   1974

The Sugar Reapers or Guyana Johnny
(Subject: the struggle of the African and Indian Sugar-Workers of
    Guyana, South America, against British Imperialism in 1953)
Production: Leipzig Opera House (world première)   1966
Radio Version — Radio DDR   1968
Production — Tartu Opera House (Estonia, USSR)   1969
Production — Odessa Opera House, USSR   1973
Radio Version — B.B.C.   1976

Joe Hill: The Man Who Never Died
(Subject: the life and death of the American proletarian revolutionary,
    Joe Hill, composer and singer of songs, in the U.S.A., 1915-16)
Production — Deutsche Staatsoper Berlin (world première)   1970
Radio broadcast of entire opera — B.B.C.   1979